MysterE Invites You...

To take part in the biggest magic trick ever played.

Start on Page One and Don't Read Ahead.

Are You Ready to BE Amused?

AMUSEMENT PARK

Start on Page One – And Do Not Read Ahead.

THE GAME IS CHANGE

AMUSEMENT PARK

Start on Page One – Do Not Read Ahead.

Copyright © 2018 - Mr. E Dan Smith III

Published By: EASEup, Life is Heart
Boulder, Colorado 80305

All Rights Reserved.
ISBN: 978-0-692-05674-5

Are You Agreeable?

My Agreeable Amusers, In Gratitude:

Miranda Love Truffle Magic Miller, Chief Alchemist Tom Boaman,
Meera Break My Heart, Lisa I Walk Wormley, Anya the Sage Smith,
Jeffrey I Am Love Krumholz, Jimy I Am Thrivin' Murphy, Dustin
Mystic Artist Brunson, Ethan Hoover on UnSplash —
and our Beloved Dog, Kiva.

Plus, the Entire River House MysterE School Community.

I Always Say Yes to

My Heart.

Whenever

I think,

"No

Way."

I Remember,

"It's already done."

Yes, we remembered Magic.

Before every thing and one, was gone.

I have a passport to guide me; yes, I now see,

To pull off the greatest Magic trick ever, on humanity.

For once we build Amusement Park, every one will come.

To un-re-remember what they have been hiding from.

We are going backward to learn what we forget.

We agree to agree to use Obvious Magic

To trick us all into Amusement.

All is Provided For Now

AP4, Now

Yes.

AMUSEMENT PARK

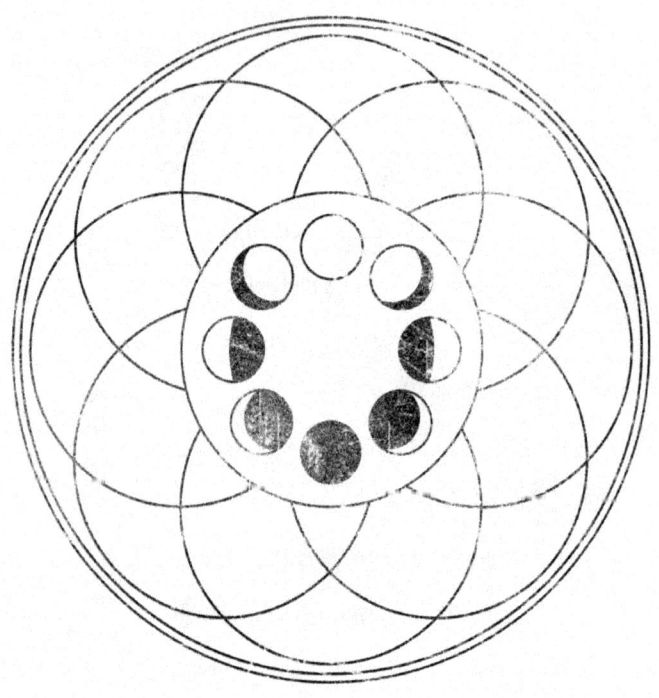

Page 2 - I Am Agreeable

Be Aware

The material you are about to read, is life altering.
For you will be unable to un-read, this literary offering.

The material is coded - to un-ravel your conditioning ahead.
You can not reject this once, you have read past, what is said.

There is absolutely nothing, anyone can do about it, there or here.
You might also likely lose everything, you think you hold so dear.

Your accustomed ways of living now, may fade, and wash out.
There is no returning canal, railway, passage or safety route.

Deny this book, maybe you deny life's agreeable offer.
Skim this book, and maybe life, skims a bit softer.

There's no way to cheat & no way to fail.
No way to succeed. No other trail.

Pour your self into this charade.
And agreeably, magical bread is made.

AMUSEMENT PARK

THE GAME IS CHANGE

BE Aware.

Turning this page cannot be undone.

Are You Agreeable?

AMUSEMENT PARK

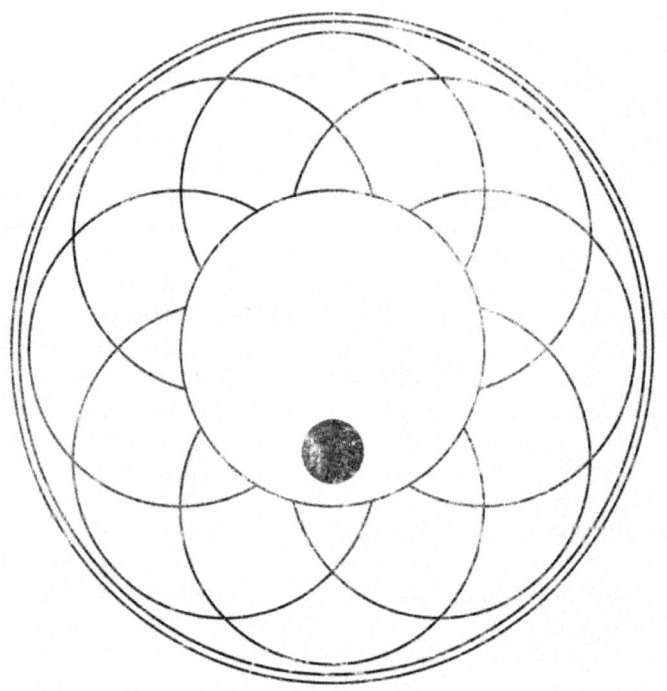

Page 6 - I Am Agreeable

The Amusement Park Theme

Résistance de Libération.

A 4Act Play, *We do spawn.*

AMUSEMENT PARK

You are walking in the woods, without a plan.

Suddenly and strangely, you bump into a man. His eyes are shining like diamonds, and his hair is kind of long. He looks right through you, and in your heart, you hear his song:

> *Every-thing is working out right,*
> *Every-thing is coming round fine,*
> *Every-thing is turning... into Light.*

Looking at your book, he says in an offhanded way:

> *I see you have a passport to the 4-Act, Amusement Park, play.*

He motions with his staff, and cries,

> *AP4! Just ahead, and right this way!*
> *Enjoy your destiny and follow the signs.*

"Hey, what's this about?" You say.

He responds:

> *I'm not allowed to reveal more about the neighbor-hood,*
> *It's all for you in that very fine book.*

He says, disappearing in the wood.

Oh, so you are still reading.

Perhaps, you are a new player in the park, and perhaps your heart said yes, to a more compassionate bark.

Well consider this: Just like entering any other establishment, there are *certain* ways; very certain ways to play:

4 Magic is undeniably **Agreeable**.

They all agree, to say.

Better be precise and bring your whole truth. A good trick requires more than a beginner's spoof. So come offering frankincense and mirth, for the biggest human disappearing act, on Planet Earth.

You are invited to read the Introduction to make your mark, of investigating, your free will choice, to enter Amusement Park.

The only thing required is simply, to leap. For it is time to un-snooze, from obvious sleep.

If at any time you don't agree to agree, then simply put the book down and let it be.

Know however, were you to either accidently or intentionally finish the introduction – you are absolutely agreeable to the grand seduction, and therefore agreeable to every word in the production.

Be true to yourself, and don't fall into the fire.

So to be even more precise, here at the wire…

THE GAME IS CHANGE

Make Only the Agreements You Plan to Keep.

AMUSEMENT PARK

Are you still reading?

Are you really aware?

It's one thing to agree, and another,

Not to care.

AMUSEMENT PARK

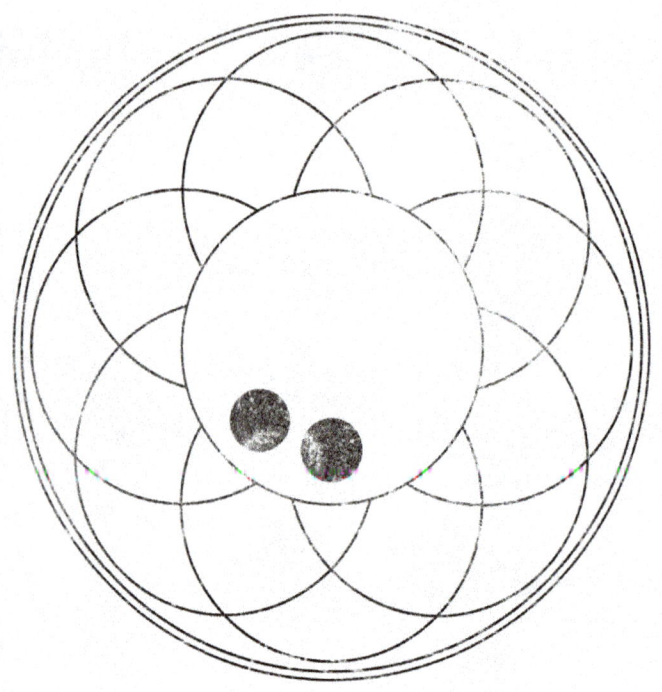

Page 14 - I Am Agreeable

Introduction to Our Play:

Are You Open to the Possibility of Magic?

Scene One: *Willing to say Yes!*

January 2018.

Here I am – still here at the River House. Of that, I am fairly quite certain – however, wondering, what else, is behind the curtain.

Oh, pardon me. Yes, yes, you are just now joining me and I've been here all along. Sometimes I forget you haven't yet heard my song.

Well, allow me to give you the simple background instructions, so we can all move into the Amusement Park, under construction. I say it this way, because even I – authoring this book – have no idea where we are flowing, in this babbling river brook…

I know as much about Amusement Park as you. *Am I the only one of us, who has the Choiceless Choice, to follow through?*

All I know is it happened in a flash. I was one minute sitting on a bench, and the next writing the first amusing stash. Only now have I paused long enough to bring in the perspective of background information; to properly set up this amusing, literary narration.

There I was: October 2009.

Nine years ago, something vast in me began to un-whirl; through an experience of love – the kind that changes worlds. I was hanging out with a woman named Bee – exploring the doorways of life's great mystery. One day, as I was speaking about things that would shift, she exclaimed, "Let's find a place, for you to be, in your gift!"

Within 24 hours, we were standing at the River House. Only problem was – Bee wasn't my spouse.

I immediately saw a vision of opportunity – An Evolutionary Center for Change, and a surrounding community. I then said, with a bit of a pride swallowing:

"Why don't you rent it, and along I'll come following."

The magic started to blossom, as all of my resistance faded in pleasure, and I soon came stumbling along, for a greater adventure.

The River House sits on a few acres, right on South Boulder Creek. Only 30 feet from me it flows, week to week. The Rocky Mountains jut up and out, from the prairie – a lonely mile from where I am narrating.

Deer, bear, mountain lions and a family of raccoons – also foxes, minx, horses and coyotes howling at the moon. It's a place of impeccable delights and incredible feeling. It has everything a person could want from nature's play of beauty and healing.

Soon thereafter, Bee and I published the Evolutionary Guidebook together, and then, we built the Evolutionary Forgiveness Labyrinth together. And these two pieces of art, have touched, many lives.

To this, I have been agreeable.

Yes, I moved almost straight from my family with spouse, into living with Bee, at the now esteemed, River House. I was moved by something, I couldn't resist. Something, I was clumsily learning to be, in agreement with.

There was a lot of hurt and confusion, in my rear view. For I found myself caught up in something, *I was never going to do.*

Fast forward: December 2012.

Then, three years later, I left Bee for the Sky Temple, for I knew my relationship with River House wasn't so simple. I absolutely had to leave – to follow my heart without knowing, where it would lead.

I had been invited to live in a budding community several miles to the north – and it was a little too far, to go back and forth.

Bee said: "If you leave me and you leave this land - you can never come back to either of us. Understand?"

And I had to leave, as you must already know – to experience the heartbreak, of the family, I had let go.

Fast forward: April 2014.

The sheriff had just left us alone in the Sky Temple.

I was sitting in the extravagant living room of the 10,000 square foot mansion in which I had been squatting for the last five weeks with Supertramp, inside the gated community miles above the city of Boulder.

Supertramp is bearded, softer and taller. I am clean shaven, pointed, and smaller. We are the same, but different somehow. He is quiet – and I like to go on, as long as allowed.

We had both recently figured out we were life artists - our new gifts, we were learning to harness.

A, *Day One*, kind of affair.

Supertramp had no money, a wearing medical condition, and was new to the scene. I had the change from the basin of our wishing well I did clean: Eight dollars – all in quarters by the way, an old car with an 1/8 tank of gas, and nowhere particular to stay.

With simple compassion, we had convinced the powers at play, we would leave the estate with some aid… and that's how we orchestrated hotel room, moving truck, and storage unit to be paid.

We avoided a felony and an immediate boot – for now we had 36 hours to shift through *not-obvious-yet* loot.

As I sat there with the truck backed up to the garage, it became clear the last act was complete, while the next is a mirage.

I thought to myself… This ought to be interesting. What could possibly be next?

An entire community had enjoyed a magical ride at the Sky Temple. We made a wishing well, built a labyrinth, planted gardens – and a paradigm shift, we penciled. We hosted parties, ceremonies and teachers from all around the world, planning we would eventually purchase the soil.

However, when it was learned our landlord had not been paying the mortgage and a bank sale was eminent, the five people in the community fractured, leaving Supertramp and I, the only ones in it.

Supertramp & I agreed to ride the play on a little bit farther. And the other faction agreed that moving out and getting the deposit back, was obviously much smarter.

Curiously, the division fell along traditional lines of have & have not: The *have* faction with chips in the game, wanted to move on. And, the *have not* faction, wanted to see what else could be spawned. The fifth community member tried to take both paths, and finally sided with the *haves*.

What an interesting play. Isn't that a bit like, our current state of affairs, today?

Supertramp and I were curious if there was, more to our story. Because the Sky Temple, still felt like our, residential laboratory. So I began imaging a solution where we all got what we wanted, by asking one simple question: *How can the haves get their deposit back, and the have-nots, receive another session?*

In imaging this, I received a vision to create exactly that result. A vision that did not include, resisting the *haves*, or ever giving up. What I saw, was some sort of catapult.

I couldn't see it all, and it mostly just felt right. It was enough, to keep me up at night. So I shared these visions with Supertramp, and then we both agreed to agree – to carry on and shine our light. That somehow together, we would wander ahead. That somehow together, we would have good meals, conversations, and safe places to lay our heads.

It would work out perfectly for everyone, we agreed to agree. We started making plans – the power would stay on, and we wouldn't need a key.

So Supertramp and I, with what little we had been loaned – rented a small truck and loaded into it, what little we owned.

We then drove around a few corners and parked before the move out inspection. Just maybe we left a window open, before our illusionary self-ejection.

When we went back to certify all tenants had retired, no doubt. A thorough inspection of the house, concluded we had in fact, all moved out.

We all said our *goodbyes*, and our *take cares*. The *haves* got their deposit back, and then drove down the mountain, unawares.

Supertramp and I followed in my old car and split a burrito at a café. And then, sensing our coast was clear – drove back up discussing our fears on the way. Under the darkness of night, we moved back on the mountain – and we threw our last coins, into our wishing well fountain.

And that's how we ended up in this startling predicament: Of squatting in a mansion and riding the Arc of Resistance.

Before I relate what happens next, a brief intermission for effect.

Allow me to tell you, what I know, about Amusement Park.

Like any place on Planet Earth, there are certain agreements to keep to remain in harmony with your environment. Spoken and unspoken in someone else's home — there are agreements to keep, less disturb the equilibrium.

In a foreign country with passport in hand, you agree to laws, customs, and currency for return to your land. Amusement Park is the same, but on a different scroll. Here, there are no laws, and no one in control.

In the Amusement Park, we all make agreements we all agree to keep. You are the warden and the prisoner, guarding the truth that you seek. *Be Aware,* for after the Amusement Park leap, the price for learning can get well — quite steep.

You will meet other characters in the play, with whom you can communicate — if you relate, with what they say.

Amusement Park is akin to a brand new nation, entirely built from compassionate creation. Amusement Park has its own customs, guidelines, currency and language.

The only thing AP4 lacks, is physical boundaries.

You'll be required to use your imagination until you get the hang of the Play.

And then a new reality appears, in your right o' way.

AMUSEMENT PARK

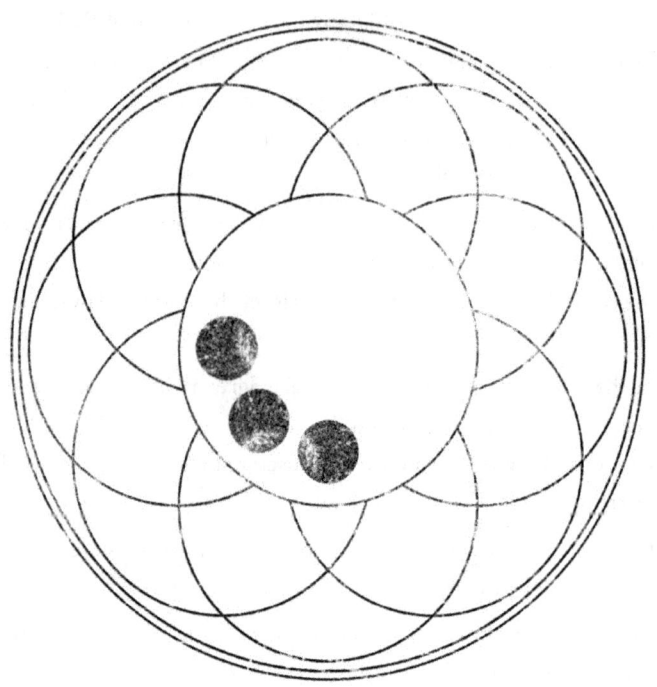

Page 22 - I Am Agreeable

Introduction to Our Play:

Are You Open to the Possibility of Magic?

Scene Two: *Follow the Signs*

Oh, We've arrived at a signpost:

AMUSEMENT PARK

Be

Aware:

Slow Down.

One Way Please.

Amusement Park Ahead:

BE

Aware.

Once you

Enter, You

Never Leave.

Hey I get it – sometimes we ignore the signposts and enter lands of a "No Trespassing" zone, with the awareness that we are willing to risk the potential repercussions for a greater adventure, into the unknown.

That is exactly what Supertramp and I were doing.

We had been asked to leave the Sky Temple five weeks earlier. We had even presented the illusion we would leave. And then, we returned under disguise, and lived there rent free.

We felt strongly we were meant to be there – that there was a higher intelligence to be played. So we stayed and we stayed and we stayed.

We set up our rooms and kitchen with our meager possessions at our secret mountain refuge. We then explored the lands, hunting for gold in the creeks, scoured by a recent deluge.

And then the most fantastical things started happening to us, and are still happening today. We faced our fears at night – and then we prayed. We faced the projections of our friends and our family's remiss, and then went beyond everything familiar, into an abyss.

We made an agreement.

Do you remember this?

If you are reading this poetry line – it means you have passed and become agreeable with, the **Be Aware / Slow Down** shrine. Take a moment to consider you might be stealing. Be in touch with exactly what, you now are feeling.

You are aware of something mysterious and unknown. What is your mood? Do you turn back, or intentionally travel on through?

Now, you see another signpost ahead.

The woods are becoming overgrown. Keep walking/reading, as in your heart, you are so prone.

Does this feel right to continue, on your own?

You can, read more words, and you can, still turn around,

However, remember, not to un-read,

While considering entering, the AP4 grounds.

Be

Alert,

Thine Book

Is your Passport.

Keep it Confidential.

BE

Alert:

Sharing

Premature,

Makes AP4 Inert.

Now a twist in the pathway, there are more obviously ahead as you advance. Can we agree to be agreeable together, for our dance?

Agreeable?

If you are still reading this literary coaster,

It means you have agreed to go into the beyond;
Past the **Be Alert** sign; a very clear poster.

Take a moment: Close your eyes and imagine the scene.
Are you in touch with what this is revealing?
Well, what are you, *really*, feeling?

Breathe deep into the sensations.
Do you feel like continuing?

One sign said; to **Be Aware** is essential,
And the other said; better keep it confidential.

It sounds like maybe you are being asked to keep a secret.
"Can you really, keep these agreements?"

For when you make & keep the agreements you speak.
You unlock the potency of amusing mystique.

And, when you are agreeable, with the AP4 play,
The more potent the magic, coming your way.

I promise you, Supertramp and I were aware that trespassing was a felony. And that driving through coded gates and squatting in a mansion could bring us all kinds of misery. We were also aware, it was quite simple. No next step had appeared in the obvious; so it felt right to stay at Sky Temple.

So to be clear: There were known and unknown repercussions of our choice; potentially delightful and painful – yet we followed our heart's voice.

We felt guided until we received further instructions – from whom and how, we were not entirely certain. For our lives were under some kind of evolutionary reconstruction. A few old friends drove up to the house to convince us to leave; that what we were doing was wrong, and only bad things we could achieve.

However, one person had a different take for our crew. He said, "I know your heart and trust what you feel, is best for you."

I said, "Thank you Professor, when the signs point me in another direction, I'll be sure to make a careful course correction."

Present Day:

So, here I am writing this 4-Act play – giving it to you as it comes my way. Some of this is background reconstruction, and other words are AP4 instruction. Oh, I wish I knew how this thing is structured – just keep reading with me, until it's uncovered.

And, let me assure you in an amusing way – that these signs are truth for you today.

For what now are you noticing anew? Remember to be aware of what you are feeling. Are you sure you want to continue?

Remember to go forward, and always with care. Agree to slow way down – for what's to come, is only in there.

You sense the Amusement Park, just ahead. *AP4 Now!* cried out the man in the woods. Is there hidden meaning in these literary goods?

So keep walking and reading – as it resonates in your heart with joy. And keep asking the question:

"Does this feel in harmony with my heart, to employ?"

Because I am, is not interested in anything below you my friend, only agreeability with what comes a 'round the river's bend.

I trust you know on some level you want to go into Amusement Park this instance – and on another, stop reading and go back to your existence.

That choice point is coming soon.

Inside themselves, everyone knows when to risk the signposts for warning – and when to heed them as an indication, for soaring.

Perhaps you can see every person's choice is truthfully unique. And there's nothing anyone can do about it, except truthfully speak. Perhaps you can see, the people trying to talk us into 'obeying' the rules – were simply exhibiting their own fears about what might happen, were they in our school.

And they weren't – nor did they know what I was feeling in my heart. They couldn't have imagined the coming fruits of such an unconventional, fresh re-start.

So their counsel was merely a projection of an agreement to

conformity in the other direction. I chose to trust my heart and for love to prevail – which brings us back to where we left off, in our little tale.

So, there I was. The sheriff had just left us alone at the Sky Temple. We had 36 hours to leave or risk jail – it was pretty simple. Without out a forethought, I picked up my phone on inspiration, and texted Bee without hesitation: *"Are you ever leaving that River House?"*

Bee's response: *How did you know?*

By reading/walking further with this voice,

You agree to accept what happens to you.

And it's absolutely by choice.

No one else can make it for you.

No one else can assist.

You are traveling alone.

There is no one to speak to,

Do you get the AP4 gist?

Up ahead another sign marker. Beyond the post, a very light trail leading into a narrowing; much darker.

> *BE*
>
> *Awake:*
>
> *Always Use*
>
> *Language that*
>
> *Other Amusers Speak.*
>
> *BE*
>
> *Awake.*
>
> *Conversing*
>
> *With Amusers*
>
> *Can 'Ever Be Faked.*

Hmmmm, so what to do with this opportunity — standing at the edge of an eternity.

There's some kind of mystery ahead, just in advance. It's impossible to predict. Are you willing to take a chance?

Therefore, I will give it to you straight — so *the Absolute Yes*, becomes your fate. It's a lot better than the old nagging voice, "I wonder what it have been like, had I made a different choice?"

Now, you might be tempted already, to question this book. Or perhaps break an agreement by being a crook - overlooking an absolute truth:

You are already agreeable, to becoming, Amused.

And, yet perhaps you're unsure of the agreements that are to come. You ask: "Is there anyway to *not* notice, and *still* play dumb?"

Or perhaps you don't like this bet of agreeing to agreements, you haven't even heard of yet.

And, these signposts are nebulous at best. How is it possible to agree with less than, an educated guess?

And what about the person who suggested you read this script. In their communication, were they a bit tight-lipped?

What is their role in the answer to your prayers? And how on earth, does one connect with the other AP4 players?

I am inviting you to notice your resistance and intrigue and to keep on exploring with your belief. For we're now beyond the assumption you have agreed to agree.

So you might as well go further at this early hour. Reading Amusement Park just might increase your power. It might also be life is more fun with agreements and signs. And better still, with new evolutionary guidelines. You, yourself, could set yourself up, to be free. And with these statements, you agree to agree.

Like when the game of basketball added the shot clock and the 3-point lines – in the face of tremendous resistance from people stuck in their whines. Basketball evolved to be better – as the game, followed the signs.

Are ready for a new playing field for life – for all those willing to venture beyond strife – to co-create something magnificent and truly beyond: *A world where we all get, what we all want.* One beyond the boundaries of confining courts, yet grounded right here, on Mother Earth.

Better read those last lines, once more, and again. For it's what we all agree to agree with, that manifests my friend.

And you may get temporarily lost, and you may get confused. Just remember, by the time you finish – you are agreeably amused. So absurdly amused at the human play, that you see those things you have hidden from yourself, until this moment, now today.

You may even discover something far greater than you can conceive. Allowing everyone on Planet Earth, to easily receive. Bringing the mystery to all of us here – all backgrounds and races. An Intelligence that connects, heals, creates and embraces. Revealing when we all lay our cards down: **We are each, incredibly holding, five Aces.**

You begin agreeing with this Intelligence and then quite suddenly – your heart reveals a pathway that is trustworthy. A view of a collective vision becomes emergent and more importantly, your role in a human convergence.

In a weird way, I've been there and now I am back. I have blazed an amusing trail – a far less, unpredictable track. And, I've collected some tools and artifacts from places beyond, to make your journey more efficient, rewarding and fond.

I present you with a piece of art to unwrap your gifts, and then serve humanity, in a way that lifts.

It took 7x7+1 for me to agreeably hear the chime. May you now have the power to become amused in far more efficient time. 7 Years, 7 months, 7 Weeks, 7 Days, or 7 Seconds. You alone are in charge of when your heart beckons. It's a sum quotient of vision, humility, desire and intent – that opens the dog door into a more compassionate establishment.

In my imagination, by precisely following these Passport directions, things become absurdly amusing in their perfect connections. And these qualifications that I blessed myself to calving, can initiate a peaceful worldly transition, into more human having.

We are now here together and it is natural in these spaces, to be nervous as you go beyond the signs to truly notice, human faces.

Enjoy these musings, as I conclude – and may Amusement Park, leave you completely *amused*.

lovE

PS: *What now? Are you really ready to play?*

If you choose to put this book down and forgo the Amusement Park, place it somewhere obvious so another fool, can embark.

See You in the Amusement Park.

AMUSEMENT PARK

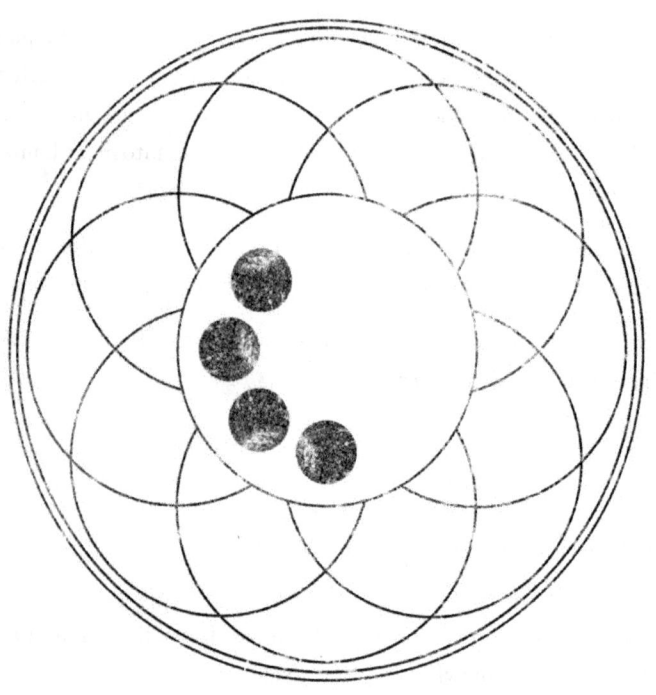

Page 36 - I Am Agreeable

Introduction to Our Play:

Are You Open to the Possibility of Magic?

Scene Three: *A Magic Trick!*

Oh, by the way, one particular note.

When the Sheriff arrived with the property owner's agent in an uproar, threats of violent physical harm were made, and then even more. The sheriff decided to wait outside with what was at stake, to see which pathway everyone would take.

Supertramp and I simply sat still with the dissidence, until it was clear to all, we were in a field of non-resistance. In that moment cleared out did the fog, when said representative became agreeable to dialogue.

We then sat down together and after stumbling a bit – we were able to listen and speak freely, about all of our its.

It was in this space that compassion entered, when the woman who said our legs would be broken became quite tender. She then commenced to cry, and suddenly became our new ally.

Poof! A Magic Trick.

The same person who was hostile moments ago, was now the sweetest soul who genuinely wanted to streamline our flow.

She offered a hotel room to Supertramp, and moving expenses for us both; then notified the sheriff to hold back charges for 36 hours, as long as we would board an agreed upon boat.

So that's the true story of the sinking of the Sky Temple ship – and how Supertramp and I came to be sitting there on the last day of our mountain space trip.

Our community members simply wanted to move on.

Supertramp and I felt strongly we were to stay. We rode their energy out and something else back in that day –

Because…

We believed all those wishes we threw into the wishing well. The magic was still brewing as far as we could tell.

We believed all the prayers we made about owning it one day. So we did the only thing we could possibly do: Press, now, re-play.

We stayed after the community split. And we stayed when people became upset and begged us to quit. And we stayed in spite of the nightmares of the sheriff and jail. And we stayed until a zero space opened up along our rails.

It was by riding this train into amusing states of non-resistance, we recognized we were bringing a new reality, into existence. Completely vulnerable and real in the face of our fears, with the sheriff literally waiting outside, scratching his ears. Then suddenly the character of our adversary went up in embers. Changed into an angel with tears.

Poof! A magic trick. Remember?

Yes! This is the space, Supertramp and I are sitting in now. The empty moving truck is backed up to the garage, and the owner and sheriff just left.

Supertramp says. "What in the name of all things amazing just occurred? "I'm not certain of anything," I say – my speech a bit slurred.

We are laying down on the couches exhausted by the exhibition, and elated by the change in our momentary condition. And this brings us back to the texting with Bee, beforehand I mentioned. Remember?

AMUSEMENT PARK

I text: *Are you ever moving out of that River House?*

Immediately her response: *How did you know?*

I respond: *Know what?*

Bee's next text, was a punch: *I terminated my lease this morning. I'll be out at the end of the month.*

It was our very first communication since I left the River House 18 months ago on permanent vacation. Minutes later, the landlord takes my call and agrees to a verbal lease. "Don't worry about the deposit, pay the rent when your income does increase."

As I hang up the phone from receiving the River House once more, I recognize the impossible has showed up again at our front door. Something was initiated by riding the Arc of Resistance out in this way. As I became more agreeable through my heart, amazing things did display.

My phone rings. It's the mother of my children.

She's looking for a place for the family to station, while their home is getting a new foundation. Our dates align perfectly; Oh, what an occasion!

So, we all move into the River House together. Me, my children, their mother, and her new man. A divinely orchestrated forgiveness journey – as we all live together and fall in love, all over again.

In the months that follow a community is born as new people arrive drawn to the fun. Supertramp paints by the river while Kiva our beloved miracle dog, lays in the sun.

Others arrive with a similar vision; to evolve the old ways we create, heal and provision. We begin with our group's mission – a way to kindly re-tool. We give birth to the inaugural River House MysterE School. Our first agreement to help us all shift:

> *The River House Community is a tribe of life artists,*
>
> *empowering everyone to be in their gift.*

This agreement has given birth to so much since then; bands, schools, art, labyrinths, books, stories, ceremonies, temples, a yoga studio and more. Magical people, situations and adventures started showing up at the door.

And that's my presentation of the information, so you can make a literary summation – to read further to join us in the Amusement Park creation.

Present Day: January 2018.

Still at the River House writing this book, I am standing with you at the beginning of a promising overlook. You have all the required background and stories – and now we look together yonder to explore new territories.

So, as you are still reading with me all this way … 9 years after it all began – we begin again, this play.

Oh, look ahead. Another signpost.

BE

Ample:

Agree There

Is Beyond Enough

For Everyone on Earth.

BE

Ample.

Agree AP4

Fashions Your

Life as an Example.

Now hang on a second, did you sit with that sign like never before? Did you open up to the realm of possibility of alchemy in store? Did you feel the column of light all around? Did you feel energy through your feet and into the ground?

For the best of your Amusement Park experience, I invite you to be open to the mysterious. By spending time opening your heart with feeling – to the space the *not-obvious-yet*, is revealing.

So are you really quite certain, you want to see beyond the curtain? Because to see further than the perception of illusionary fabric, you must be open to the possibility of magic!

Now paws – turn around, and before you go ahead. Did you happen to notice what the back of the good sign said?

I

Am,

An Absolute

Yes! I Am Committed

To the

Journey.

Into The

AP4 Abyss

Feel into the truth of what the words on the sign have said. And since you cannot un-read what you have read, impress them upon your heart instead.

Perhaps my friend, our evolutionary learning curve is simply an arc — an invisible arc we ride over and over in splendor, until we never give up and always surrender. This current simply wants to take us all somewhere new, and all early exits place us back exactly in queue. However when we train our awareness to ride even farther, we find a portal out of one reality and into another.

Let me assure you as we set our sails, no-thing is certainly how love prevails. No-thing is how we participate in the collaborative insanity, of pulling off the greatest magic trick on humanity.

We agree to agree to learn to ride the Arc of Resistance, by being agreeably agreeable to going the distance. This allows us to become the change, rather than resistance. Then we share it with others, to become agreeably efficient.

This is how we change the characters in the play. All of them — one by one, and day by day.

For when we meet humans with listening and compassion, masks dissolve and paradigms shift. Our adversaries become our helpers, and one by one, we assist. We co-create field of human potential — which draws everyone in through its compounding principle.

Because already we have agreed to agree in obvious knowing — this planet is abundance and completely overflowing. We see there are more empty hotel beds on any given night, than there are folks in a bed-less plight. We know that enough food is thrown out on every single shift, for restaurants to put the plates outside for the hungry to lift. We recognize there is already enough of all things – to ensure no one wonders if the basics, tomorrow brings.

So our intent is with our exemplary compassion, that hoarding and empty estates simply go out of fashion. And what now is en vogue as the collective fixation, becomes favorable to a more compassionate inclination.

To this we can mostly certainly agree to agree.

Because when the Amusement Park we are creating appears – everyone gets a glimpse into new frontiers.

Do you remember?

Amusement Park is an accelerator; a most efficient Evolutionary Guide. Because my friends – **All is Provided 4** – now inside.

We Embark, for Amusement Park!

AP4 exists first in our Hearts, and then on our lands.

Then we build all over the **world**, as efficiently as we can.

Through a process of **un-for getting** what we have done,

We agree to agree, it has agreeably, already begun.

For Amusement Park, We Embark!

AMUSEMENT PARK

!Poof!

A natural process of transformation
Has begun. For 1+1+1+1 does not equal four,
1+1+1+1 = 1+2+4+8, which is a compounding score.
The gateway into a much larger tune,
Now caterpillars at cycle's end,
Our essence changing soon.
Imagine.
Where we are going,
There is no war on drugs.
There is no us against them,
No one is alone, or above giving hugs.
No one fears new doors, death, or deportation,
Where we are going there's a passport
with simple explicit instructions.
We all play together and there is always a bed,
A nourishing meal and beautiful conversation to be had.

!Poof!

THE GAME IS CHANGE

!Poof!

Now we are becoming butterflies,

Because each one of us agreed to agree,

On a new set of guidelines designed, to set humanity free.

No one gets left behind, and they all come along.

Their timeline, just a bit different than thee.

One day we all sing together, a song.

Until then,

Your journey starts alone -

There's no way to fall behind.

Clues and signs and Amusers ahead;

A treasure hunt of the most extraordinary kind.

Successful? Perhaps not, in the place you come from.

However, I promise in here, everything you

Can possibly imagine, is already done.

We all play together and there is always a bed,

A nourishing meal and beautiful conversation to be had.

!Poof!

AMUSEMENT PARK

THE GAME IS CHANGE

_____
_____
_____
Book #: _____

                           The River House Cook
                           c/o The MysterE School
                           1491 S Foothills Highway.
                           Boulder, CO 80305

I Am in the Amusement Park

This book,

I agree to finish,

To ride Noah's Arc.

I agree by reading further,

I make agreements, I intend to keep.

I agree to my commitment of being agreeable,

4 Divine Intelligence, orchestrates everything I speak.

Allowing all Amusers – yes, me too to receive.

I agree that when, we agree this way.

It is done, like we have agreed.

It being my heart's desires.

It being my healing.

It being my joy.

It being;

Me in my highest potential, and completely amused.

I Agree to be Agreeable while I am in the Amusement Park, and I am relieved of this Agreement, when I climb aboard the Arc.

Name _____   Date _____

        X_____

Now,
Sign that last page.
1st Read Completely Aloud.
Tear it out of your book.
Tri-fold; it's self-addressed.
Mail2: River House Cook.
There, he'll stir up a brew,
Amusing us all - even,
You.
We will follow up with instructions on how to connect.
Maybe the US Mail, to slow things down and reflect.
There's a much larger play coming so soon.
We send you instructions and clues.
For Amusement Park is growing.
Beyond our current simple newsletter.
An evolving idea for a forum, much better.
New currency & the design of a time bending station.
Amusers of all kinds will bring these into our imagination.
Until we hear from you with your gift,
And you hear back from us,
Venture into the tunnel.
Be keenly aware of a swirling funnel.
Keep on going, as long as you are Agreeable.

AMUSEMENT PARK

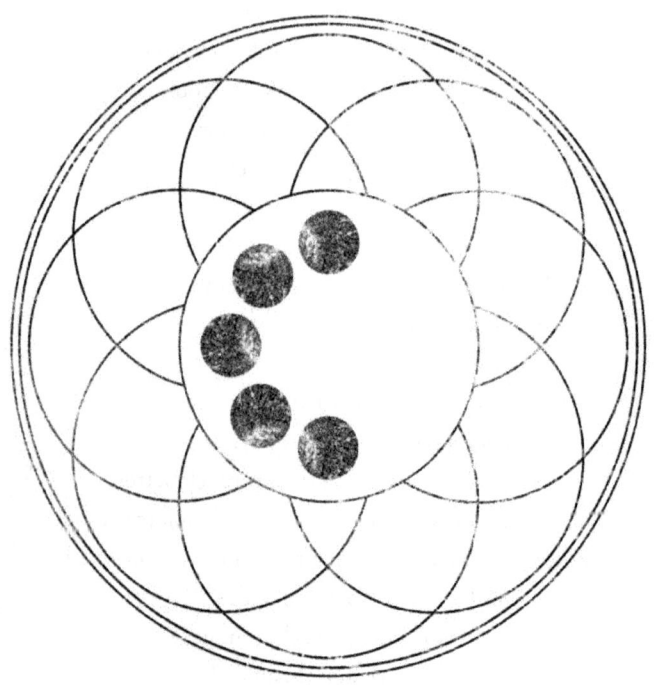

Page 52 - I Am Agreeable

ACT I: *Portal of Entry*

Scene One: *Remember to Remember*

Well, you signed up for the ride. You've committed to the trip. Come with me on our efficient time travel space ship. Have you paid your entrance fee?

It's $8 of course. Wait a minute… You thought this was free?!

In exchange you receive Amusement Park rides – to take yourself rainbowing across the sky. Imagine the tickets and imagine the loot, of millions of Amusers placing coins in one collective boot. What then becomes possible all together? Who knows, perhaps we can change, even the weather?

Let's together agree to agree in song, you consider gifting more as you play along. I'll front the $8 in quarters to you just for fun. We agree to agree, this is already done.

We agree to agree that later on in the play, something opens your heart along the way. Then you may feel inclined to gift your park fee, or perhaps make a contribution to local community.

Not through the mail, but on an electronic device. We agree to agree, that your eight dollars does suffice. We agree to agree there are no more agreements for more, unless your Heart guides you, then absolutely for sure.

We agree to agree these funds multiply, creating a much larger compassionate supply – building Amusement Parks for amusers to explore; feeding the hungry and empowering the poor

We agree to agree that in the Amusement Park – everyone is in their gift and leaving their mark. We all do what we love in this parade – and for marching, we all get handsomely paid.

Because we all have agreed that, we all play together and there is always a bed – a nourishing meal and beautiful conversation to be had:

4 Now, is never, too late.

"I Am Agreeable"

Read that statement.
Say it out loud!

Yes, I Am Agreeable!

Let's imagine together.

You are agreeable, and I Am is absolutely agreeable.
For what is the difference between One, and the same?
4 being agreeable is the amusing requirement for our play.
There are posters and agreements, ahead in plain view.
Some quite a bit more subtle, scattered and few,
Please read the right side italics slowly and aloud.
2x is the recipe for a magical brew.
Your journey is not faster,
But more efficient
4 You.

AMUSEMENT PARK

Now you are standing beyond the last signpost. There are no more. The relief of the terrain around you has narrowed. What could possibly be in store?

The woods here are thicker – wet mist like a veil. You've already been to what's behind you. Too steep each side, for any kind of trail.

On the horizon before you, a glimpse of the new moon. A tiny sliver of light on the side of a great darkened balloon. Slow down to notice in the fading light – a feeling drawing you into the emptiness outside. Is that an outline of an old wooden door, hiding behind vines, overgrowth and... Have you seen this portal before?

Perhaps if I took one more step.
I curiously say.
It's getting incredibly dark.
Still here, I am, feeling divinely guided, this way.

Despite my heart singing so loud -
Why is it - the closer I get,
The thicker the clouds?

You remember in this moment, you carry a light. Imagine earlier you put this in your pack – and suddenly, you have sight.

Ohhhhh right!
I grabbed it by accident... at the last instant.

The small head lamp which fits above your eyes, activates a knowingness deep inside.

> *I remember now! I always have sight.*
> *I simply slow down; then imagine my delight!*

Now with your new vision it suddenly occurs to you, "It is time for a thorough, passport review."

> *My Pass Port is sacred.*
> *I carry it with me at all times.*
> *For when I get confused or scared.*
> *It guides me to remember, my light and my lines.*

You are now having a faint memory that you've always been carrying this passport. Like the headlamp:

> **I've made these agreements before.**

Me and Supertramp must have remembered something to have been willing to go beyond that door. You know *that door*... the door that always seems to keep, a less-than perfect score.

Life has a way of testing us as we travel into the flow. Perhaps then it feels right to carry our passports, wherever we go. Just so you know what is in store, I've been carrying one for years – actually far more.

So let us review together what we have agreed upon to date, and then let's start building an Amusement Park, we can celebrate.

4 it is now time, for the *4 Signs Rhyme*:

Now

With Four

Signs I've Become

Agreeable. I Am Aware,

Alert, Awake, and I Am Ample.

So with Willingness, I now embark.

I Am Slowing Down, and I Am Agreeably

Agreeable Inside the Amusement Park. I Am

Communicating with Precision, Allowing a

Compassionate Agreeability to Flower

As I Remember,

I Am, That I Am;

My Light & Power.

I Say Yes to My Heart

Now as you may already know, magic works on two levels. The first level is the <u>obvious</u>. The second level is the *not-obvious-yet*.

In the obvious level of magic, someone reading this book would memorize these spells, and then repeat the words back to themselves. This someone with obvious magical decree, would most likely experience a pleasant shift in their reality.

Things would begin to flow for them in ways beyond the practical – as obvious puzzle pieces rearrange to make life magical.

For a time.

Until they are tested when the lows become so low – for the old roller coasters keep going and going and get stuck in the slow.

All of us reading here have experienced obvious magic and the let downs that quake. The *not-obvious-yet* is still not obvious, and trips us like invisible stones on the path we did take.

Then the magic is gone before we notice it's fading, and we forget the magic was ever happening at all – and before too long we are unable to see we've hit a great wall. Being lost in the Park is simply a cue, you have come across the *not-obvious-yet* in your obvious view.

That this book is transformational is obvious. Reading from your obvious mind, reaps obvious effects.

There is no way to circumnavigate, what truth reflects.

Amusement Park as it is designed, instantly activates a parallel holographic representation – of the *not-obvious-yet* for you to work with in your imagination.

It is your responsibility to see into your current obvious set, those things concealed in the *not-obvious-yet*.

In obvious magic you first trip over invisible pebbles, then bump into invisible walls – and then if you are still unable to see the obviously in visible; accidents of all kinds you befall.

Eventually your annoyance causes you to deny and conceal – the magic that once felt so incredibly real. This disagreeability re-establishes outdated agreements to create a buffer – of familiar arrangements espousing division, dis-ease, and for us all to suffer.

The trick is to activate the *not-obvious-yet* with a heart kind of marveling, so that what's currently invisible, begins *sparkling*.

Imagine you can indeed illuminate the *not-obvious-yet* fate – so the things that used to trip you up, now with you cooperate.

Feel into your Heart and use your inner vision toys – to make the **n**ot-**o**bvious-**y**et, *sparkle* – or produce **noys**.

Imagine indeed, you have the power to create *noys*.

So now, you know.

Your responsibility is simply to notice. Perceive when there is new noise in your obvious reality. You can play with the noys of sparkle, or go annoying back around the traffic circle.

Now to be responsible is different than exasperation, for there is a purpose to all this anger and frustration. Those who practice obvious magic… can become **a**gainst the **n**ot-**o**bvious-**y**et **d**omain, or anoyd…

Yes, those who become annoyed with the noise of the obvious insanity, are in resistance to change and limited in their humanity.

They talk about magic — though nothing significant ever changes. It is annoyingly revealing in all of its phases.

Yes, all our words have meaning and definition, although…

I am no Obvious Magician.

Magicians in the **n**ot-**o**bvious, or **no**; simply are blemishing their rhyme — for they are saying *"no,"* all the time. It's not their fault they are stuck, and for certain they think — very bad luck.

To this, they are agreeable.

In a moment, I invite you to go four pages back in your mind, to the moment you read the *4 **Signs**,* rhyme.

What was your level of agreeability? What level of magic do you practice, and with what durability?

So, before we deem ourselves all magicians yet, let's examine our potency and take a breath. It could use some refinement, is my less than educated guess.

Did I take Dog medicine and paws?

*Was I aware of that column of Light around me **at all**?*

Did I take the time to open my entire being to Me?

And did I, truly Agree?

Is there awareness — ANY AT ALL — that I was then,

Creating an Amusement Park, far too small?

(Perhaps we will go back to the *4 Signs Rhyme* in a bit;)

First, let us talk to the Dog and paws.

Kiva says, to illuminate the *noys*, we must become dedicated to a higher level of magic, and paws.

She says to agree with this clause.

> *I agree to open my Heart to magic.*
> *I agree this Heart Magic connects me*
> *To the Intelligence, that created all of reality.*
> *For when I Am Heart Magic immersed,*
> *I am connected to the highest form of intelligence, in the Universe.*

The incantation tone:

Om, Hrim Anahata, Guru Om

So going back to the *4 Signs* rhyme. Can you agree to agree to impress those words into your heart instead? Rather than with memorization, which you'll obviously forget with your head.

Can you agree to agree to impact the *not-obvious-yet* – so that what used to trip you up, works with you, instead?

In other words, can you agree to agree, that all the noise and *noys* in your play, simply wants to be noticed in some sort of magical way?

Can I agree that, I have been mired in an obvious and ordinary past?
Can I agree there's a filter distorting my view, I wear like a mask?
Can I agree most every human being wears one, least for show?
Can I agree it's time to remove the masks and fully let go?
Can I agree it now happens – with ease for everyone?
Can I agree in agreement that it's already done?

Without actually making specific agreements, we can open to the **Possibility of Magic** by asking questions and letting them rest.
Kiva says, "Yes, laying down is the best."

Letting things rest is an essential part of Heart Magic.
Says our beloved Dog,
I am agreeable to Divine timing and orchestration,
And unconditional Love.

Now, that's in italics and it's over to the right. My suggestion is you fashion your consciousness to be completely agreeable and speak those words out loud, and on sight.

Say them slowly with feeling and imagination; Say them with confidence you are conducting a magical spelling on all of creation.

I re-remember, by reading further, I agree to be agreeable.

AMUSEMENT PARK

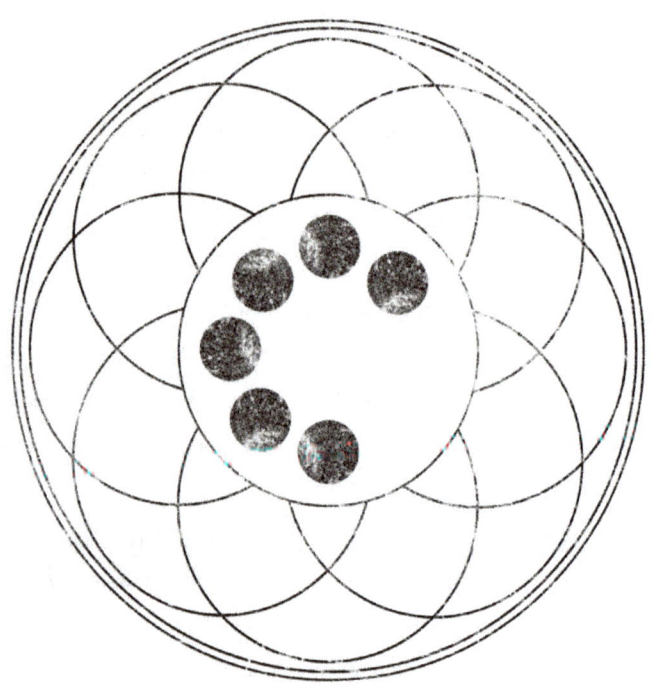

Page 64 - I Am Agreeable

ACT I
Portal of Entry

Scene Two: *Let's Take it Further.*

Now, let's take it further.

Imagine you are in the most exquisite Amusement Park ever created by the Master bark. Remember to keep slowing down and be aware of any new bench-mark.

Keep all your agreements in a way that cultivates integrity in your feeling body. Give yourself permission in your a-musings, to be rather quite gaudy.

Use the space between the lines of these paragraphs as a cue, to investigate what you have read and to what you want to add juice. Use the medicine of Dog, to paws and impress upon your being – when you feel the potency of what you are experiencing and reading. Slow Down and Be Aware.

Have I made myself agreeably clear?
Excellent to hear!

So, imagine then, AP4 or Amusement Park, reveals only what you are ready to receive at exactly the right time – and does so in the right place and perfectly in rhyme. Easily edible and most pleasantly digestible. Agree to agree that this is true; and only if only, it's only for you.

For Amusement Park creates itself first according to *your* intent, not mine. You are now in a great scavenger hunt – where absolutely nothing happens by accident, and it's always on time. In the Amusement Park you are gifted in all ways, and always with great care, for everything you could possibly require is all ways in there. To this, we agree to be agreeable.

It is then with our mutual consent, that agreements are made and kept, and about what we speak is agreeably relevant.

Possibly in a very strange way, you are beginning to suspect, that you've set yourself up well for this amusement trek.

It is already done,
For, I am the Master, of my destiny.
When in my Heart, I am One.

Now, that's in italics and it's over to the right. My suggestion is you fashion your consciousness to be completely agreeable and speak those words out loud, and on sight.

Say them slowly with feeling and imagination. Say them with confidence you are conducting a magical spelling on all of creation.

So let's imagine for a second, that the *not-obvious-yet*, is simply in the unconscious. It is what your heart and mind cannot see – and shows up for you in the Amusement Park, automatically.

You can be annoyed by the noise and stay asleep, or be a pioneer discovering sparkling clues leading you free – to this we most certainly agree to agree.

Imagine now that Amusement Park is simply giving you an efficient way to evolve, one that operates with grace, ease, and lightness of being to solve.

Imagine how much more enjoyable life would be with everyone opening their locks, rather than stumbling and tripping over rocks.

Imagine that Amusement Park reveals the *not-obvious-yet* perfectly in divine timing and flow, which by the way is already happening now, you know.

Remember?

To commit – simply be in agreement with It.
It being, the Amusement Park, of course!

Now, let's agree to agree to take it even further.

Agree to agree that you are at peace with the *Past*.

With whatever has happened,
And whomever it was with,
Whether you pulled a trigger or used your fist.
Whether you were good or bad, a celebrity or poor.
Can you imagine you, entering such a magnificent door?
Where the shame fell away and the heart opened wide,
Granting you all the wishes you are holding inside?

Now, let's agree to agree to take it even further.

Agree to agree that you are at peace with the *Present*.

With whatever is happening,
And whomever it is with,
Whether I pull a trigger or use my fist.
Whether I am good or bad, a celebrity or poor.
Can I imagine me, entering such a magnificent door?
Where the shame falls away and the heart opens wide,
Granting me every wish I am holding inside?

Now, let's agree to agree to take it, even further.

Agree to agree that you are at peace with the **Future**.

With whatever happens,
And whomever it is with,
Whether we are guided to pull a trigger or use our fists.
Whether we look good or bad, celebrities or poor.
Can we imagine us, entering such a magnificent door?
Where our shame falls away and our hearts open wide,
Granting us every wish we are holding inside?

Now, let's agree to agree to take it, even further.

Now, that we've agreed to be at **peace**. Kiva says, *Repeat after me:*

I am at peace with past, present and future.
I agree to impress this truth into my being with Heart Magic.
With this, I am agreeable and ecstatic.
Thinking won't do it — yet feeling will,
To bring the not-obvious-yet, up to be healed.

Now that's in italics and on the right, so fashion your consciousness to be completely agreeable and speak those words out loud and on sight. Say them slowly with feeling and imagination. Say them like you are conducting a magical spelling on all of creation.

AMUSEMENT PARK

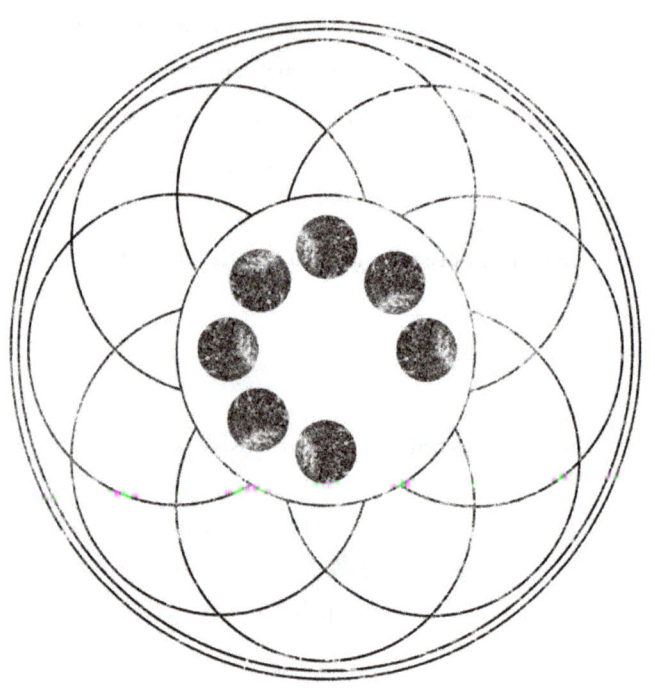

Page 70 - I Am Agreeable

ACT I

Portal of Entry

Scene Three: *The Four Realms*

Whew! You've agreed to be at peace.

The Amusement Park is noticeable. AP4 is now opening a door — because Amusement Park is absolutely *agreeable*.

Now, the ways in which you haven't been at peace before, must come tumbling down in your awareness into some future store. Together we have set something in motion; together we have consumed a most marvelous compassionate potion. A brew which brings a change of perspective abound – consisting of hidden puzzle pieces turned upside down.

And to employ the *not-obvious-yet*, we agree to train our awareness to turn them around. It's vital therefore to have a solid comprehension of the other characters in this play, to keep our energy up high, to stay.

And to assist you with our amusing play of alchemy and passion, let's review the Four Realms of Magic in this fashion.

Realm One: The Ordinary Realm

The Ordinary Realm is the very real and rational human play on Planet Earth.

The vast majority of the inhabitants of the Ordinary Realm are agreeable to the languages and cultures of an older civilization – *mine, yours, us and them, winners and losers, success and failure, healthy* and *sick, no, can't, weak, it's not my fault, you are to blame, you are wrong, guilty as charged, sin and damnation.*

Ordinary Magicians do not readily recognize magic as being relevant or real – and follow along with the rest of the herd, riding on their agreed upon wheels.

It is nearly impossible to find peace in the Ordinary Realm without a tremendous amount of desire. Desire then, is the pathway out of the Ordinary Realm cleavers. The ones with the most amount of ordinary desire, become the ordinary leaders.

Ordinary leaders naturally form groups in agreed upon causation – to form institutions of religion, finance, medicine, government, and education.

It is important to note these Ordinary Magicians use very ordinary language in making their agreements — creating for themselves a hierarchical organized system of reason: The Highest Order of the Ordinary, always in season.

The Highest Order of the Ordinary is agreeable to holding up the fabric of the collectively agreed upon reality together. It's an important job in the Intelligence's plan, to wear this feather.

As they become proficient in their ordinariness, these ordinary leaders of respect, develop the unconscious ability to float between the Ordinary Realm and the next. Becoming more aware of the obvious to solve, they unknowingly vacate the Ordinary Realm to evolve.

This usually happens between lifetimes.

Realm Two: The Obvious Realm.

In the Obvious Realm, a much smaller group of former Ordinary Magicians are becoming aware of language competence — and have begun to ask questions with obvious confidence. They learned the very basics of co-creation in ordinary schools, yet remain unaware of the entire *not-obvious-yet* truths.

These Obvious Magicians keep tripping on *invisible* things by sharing — a mask collection they cannot see they are wearing.

Masking was initiated by the suffering in the Ordinary Realm theatrical production. Everyone put them on, to deal with the chaos of the Ordinary Realm construction.

AMUSEMENT PARK

Newcomers to the Obvious Realm have no awareness of their masks, nor those of the others. As the play moves forward, ordinary parents, teachers, coaches, and pastors all help sculpt a character's druthers.

These characters get really tweaked in the Obvious Realm, as they try to move beyond the suffering at the Ordinary helm.

You see, they cannot fully un-remember what was upset back in there – for they saw Ordinary Magicians sweep obvious things under the rug, into the *not-obvious-yet* nowhere.

Obvious Magicians feel the *not-obvious-yet* as a feeling of distrust – and therefore are annoyed by the ordinary faction. This annoyance builds until it is released in a display of behavior and actions.

This disruption causes a ripple in the Ordinary Realm unpleasant to the majority's condition. Not liking the disruption, they point fingers and toss blame at the annoying Obvious Magician.

How obvious now: Obvious Magicians are being blamed for feeling something real and divisible – and how obviously important this is for the evolution of the invisible.

This projection is painful and initiates a resolve – and the shamed magician becomes obviously able to evolve. They eventually find less obvious pockets they can trust, and begin involving in group plays with more drama and lust.

Now, the evolving characters of this obvious play, appear as the difficult characters we meet each day.

These black sheep find one another and agree to agree; to herd together as a new kind of bourgeoisie. And by now it must be obvious to you reading with overwhelm – these black sheep are the Masters of the Obvious Realm.

Their power of course is amplified in groups, which creates

instability amongst their troops. The obvious has become so painful to these magicians, they must break from the ordinary missions.

Therefore, now and obviously, the highest teachers in the Obvious Realm are the *Masters of the Obvious*. And obviously they joined together with a promise to keep: To establish a most annoying auspicious herd of the absurd. **The Order of the Black Sheep.**

These Black Sheep Magicians speak a lot about being awake and empowered – becoming teachers, songwriters, gurus and poets by the hour.

Predictably, these magicians trip over another more significant threat; for not even a Master of the Obvious can see everything in the *not-obvious yet*.

And with this dramatic and impressive fall, they place upon the Alter of the Obvious, their second to last mask: *Anger*. Anger for all.

Baaaaaaaaaaaaaaaaaaaaaa!

Those of the Order of the Black Sheep have passed more than a few critical tests of faith – and therefore faith is the obvious pathway, away from the Obvious Realm wraith.

Their most obvious challenge, to which all Black Sheep have fully agreed, is that their flock is obviously the most special of all magical breeds. This declaration of grazing in the highest of all pastures, makes their magic dangerous and slightly fractured.

So obvious it is, the Black Sheep have obscured the obvious truth.

AMUSEMENT PARK

That they have become agreeable to suspend their seeking and roost.

And of course they have, because the company these magicians like to keep – still happen to all be sheep.

Therefore, then, now and obviously: these Obviously Obvious Magicians have tricked themselves with their vow, and may be getting a glimpse of their foolishness, somehow now.

Those in the Order of the Black Sheep are so obvious, they have made it nearly impossible to leave their self-involved audience. And they were obviously agreeable along the way or it wouldn't have come to this. Perhaps, they have tricked themselves into experiencing, a far more agreeable bliss.

For this sub-culture has been able to shed most of their fleece, but not their very last mask; which upon removing would enable an Obvious Magician to be fully at peace with… wait for it…

Being a black sheep.

Now the Black Sheep Magician's obvious choice to remove the final mask shawl, is not something that can come from choice – that's too obvious of a call.

The choice to leave the Obvious Realm cannot be born of freewill. It must paradoxically come in the form of a more ominous thrill. This choice-less choice arrives through a *not-obvious-yet* vortex in their current situation, when at last it is time for their Obvious Realm graduation.

The way this happens is by the Black Sheep magic-tricking

THE GAME IS CHANGE

themselves perplexed – out of the Obvious Realm and directly into the *not-obvious-yet* realm, which is next.

By placing their faith in a relationship with a shaman of the *not-obvious-yet*, they make themselves agreeable to a not-obvious net. This medium, who obviously knows anyone engaging with a shaman is bound to trip over the *not-obvious-yet* and embarrassingly fall – is silently complicit with a watching audience and extended curtain call.

The shaman also certainly knows that those of the Black Sheep land, are somewhat likely to turn their magic around in a valiant last stand. Still the shaman is agreeable to this resistance of the these sheep, in the *not-obvious-yet* ways, they obviously keep.

The shaman's agreeability to riding the Arc of Resistance out until the end, encourages the Black Sheep to be in agreement, in *not-obvious-yet* ways they comprehend.

These shamans are aware they flow between the Obvious Realm and the next; and they do this in agreeable *not-obvious-yet* service. The learning curve is steeper in the next realm so they serve until they are so obvious, that their shamanic magic gets amusingly distributed within the Black Sheep godliness.

And by the shaman being absurdly and obviously adept, the final *not-obvious-yet* agreements from the Obvious Realm are kept.

The shaman of course, who is obviously a highly distinguished Black Sheep member – then trips over the *not-obvious-yet* as well; and is tricked in splendor.

Yes a foolish dog's heart so big, the coyote is suddenly in fashion. For how ready are Black Sheep to see their beliefs go up in ashes?

Who is truly ready to receive, such a gift?

How can one give a gift so obvious, that no Black Sheep can miss?

That gift can only come with a freewill twist:

Because the biggest magic trick on Earth, is a human Hail Mary:

> *The disappearing of the Obvious Realm,*
> *To make Magic Ordinary!*

And guess what? The Black Sheep will never choose it on their own
— obviously.

When the Obvious Realm is gone, all magicians in all realms will find the ordinary to be magical, and then everyone becomes agreeable and at peace.

To this, I am agreeable.

It is up to all of us, you see.

For the biggest disappearing act on humanity can only be exacted by the very highest Order of the Black Sheep Magicians – who have agreed to the agreeable agreement of being on the hook, to delivering said biggest trick, by reading this book.

And because we have agreed there is no un-reading, we have now agreed with all of our being.

Yes, you have enough desire **and** faith both, to get free of the Obvious Realm and grow. And the shaman who initiated this magical trickery was invited by you – you know?

THE GAME IS CHANGE

Yes, you.

You invited me here.

You are co-writing this play.

To go   backward   in time.

To re-member. To put back together.

To agree to agree, to remember as lyrical.

No more   spelling   in the dark,

For you my friend, are a miracle.

And you my friend,

Invited your-

Self into Amusement Park.

AMUSEMENT PARK

I Am Invited my bark,
Right into Amusement Park.
The joke I now do plainly see,
Lands directly on, yours truly.
I tricked myself into being here now.
& I travel with passport & light somehow.
Because, it being my first day and all,
I am bound to be in the spaces
Between the old cell wall
And this agreeable
New shawl.
So now,
I am agreeable
to cast only
Compassionate
Spells for all of evolution,
In thought, feeling, word and deed,
Into & throughout all of creation,
For all those in genuine need,
for the prayed for solution.
So that in this moment,
Bart Simpson is a poet.
All is Provided 4 Now,
in the Amusement Park Tao.

Realm Three: The Realm of Possibility.

In the Realm of Possibility, magicians are dedicated to becoming compassionate by riding the Arc. We willingly learn to use the spells of an emerging compassionate reality with the full cooperation of the Intelligence to activate the Amusement Park.

As Compassionate Magicians, we learn to be agreeable with the Intelligence in speak – because we have experienced when we are not agreeable, the learning is, well – quite steep.

We agree to agree to remain humble in this education – for with this awareness comes the power of creation. We agree to agree that life plays best when we ask from the heart; therefore the more pure our desires are from the start.

Becoming *Amused* is the game for the magician entering the Realm of Possibility. A Compassionate Magician therefore becomes comfortable in humility.

With this compassionate awareness, we see how each of us is individually the center – of an infinite benevolent Universe, our mother, our mentor. We agree then to take the responsibility, to remain agreeable in every realm we engage as foreseeable.

We agree to agree to use Heart Language in all of our agreements, conversations and thoughts, and we agree to agree that we can never be bought. All Compassionate Magicians agree to give thanks – that our gifts emerge and are valuable to all ranks.

We agree to agree that wherever we go, we are on course – that we are protected, guided and cared for by an agreeable Source.

AMUSEMENT PARK

We are agreeable to be in tune with divine orchestration, always carrying a field of non-resistant liberation. We bring benevolent vibrations wherever we are seeable. And to this we are impeccably agreeable. We are also agreeable to a self-less service jive, for Compassionate Magicians always have what we require to thrive.

Tests of compassion exist in the Realm of Possibility, as does an expanded awareness to ask for assistance – were we to find ourselves discovering more of the *not-obvious-yet* in our existence. To this we are agreeable because we agree to agree, that the learning continues onward, and onward we be.

This agreement creates strong compassionate communities of sisters and brothers, which form by being agreeable in their hearts with the Intelligence and others.

Compassionate Magicians then, are cooperatively helping one another into a collective state of amusement abound – recognizing the path for what it is, with its roller-coaster ups and downs.

The learning edge for the Compassionate Magician, is asking for help with **humility** and **transparence** – and then cultivating **gratitude** for the learning, which can certainly be pleasant.

Because we can all easily agree to agree that this learning is fun, and that all experiences are necessary in this amusing pun.

In the Amusement Park, everyone is a mirror for everyone else. We are all the **same, but different.** Compassionate Magicians assume full responsibility for who we are as human beings, and recognize that all magicians in all realms are becoming masters of experience.

Furthermore, Compassionate Magicians are the architects of a new human reality – as we agree to agree to recognize our collective destiny. All while keeping our individual freedoms and our true identity.

And we agree to see how all magicians are learning as they grow, and when someone trips on the *not-obvious-yet*, we assist as it feels right to do so.

And this is how we agree to agree that Evolutionary Centers for Change we birth, right here on the Ordinary Magical Planet Earth.

Now that this is the biggest magic trick around.

Perhaps, we can agree to make it the only game left in town?

For how much longer can we deal with the **Obvious**,

As we are stepping in piles of dead bees on the ground?

B B B B B B B B

Our plan is simple:

Gather the Magicians of the Order of the Black Sheep and invite them to read this book – to assist them in magic tricking themselves into the Realm of Possibility, so we can all play together in the greatest disappearing act on Planet Earth – which is, wait for it....

AMUSEMENT PARK

Taking Away, the Obvious.

We will herd the remaining black sheep as only coyotes could, one by one by one by one out the obvious neighborhood – to this we agree to be agreeable.

The impact on the Obvious Realm is instantaneous. Suddenly, there is movement toward wholeness in the domain – as there is no one in the Obvious Realm to accept the ordinary blame and shame.

So a process is initiated.

As the Order of the Black Sheep Magicians become agreeable to vacate the Obvious Realm, the more assistants we have for our trick, lest we get overwhelmed. For numerous flocks of all colors are suddenly on the move – and with them all humans fall into new grooves. Everyone, in ways that are *not-obvious-yet*, has agreed to this play – for we have all agreed to receive lots of help along the way.

While shifting the entire human population, we require all able hearts to be in orchestration; to this we agreeably agree.

Realm Four: The Realm of Compassion.

In the Compassionate Realm, the magic is done in pairs of Compassionate Magicians, often between beloved partners – Twin Flame counterparts – who may or may not be intimately together in body, and most certainly are in spirit and hearts.

Regardless of physicality or not, Twin Flames are the instructors who share the essence of the magic of agreeability and have mastered the Arc of Resistance and are now able to enter Noah's Arc – the last ride in the Amusement Park.

Twin Flames then, go two by two by two by two, and we begin operating with magic that has a holographic score. For $2+2+2+2$ does not equal, $8+16+32+$*sixty-four;* it's infinitely far, far more.

Noah said '2 by 2,' which equals $2x2x2x2$, which equals a geometrically compounding equation which is ***only agreeable*** with spells of compassionate creation.

With this, all Compassionate Magicians agree to agree. And because it's amusing – let's re-agree with what we just agreed – to amuse ourselves with our own hilarity.

*Multiplistic, geometrically compounding magical equations, are **only agreeable** with spells of compassionate creation.*

It's agreeable then by all Magicians in the Park, that Light is always triumphant over Dark. Because, we agree to agree that if any of us sees anyone dimming, we open our hearts to them, to keep them shimmering.

We continue on the journey to bring compassion and possibility to the Ordinary Realm of fun. And we practice Heart Magic, until this is obviously done.

Therefore by agreeing to Noah's Arc of Resistance ride, we all easily, (one, by one, by one, by one) perfect our magic, and fall in stride.

Then we join (two, by two, by two, by two) to create a compassionate reality. We agree this is absolutely true.

We further agree to agree that everyone who is meant to come on this journey of causation, comes perfectly by free will and by divine orchestration. Which may look like each one of us acting the role of Morpheus, when we agreeably recognize a Master of the Obvious – who is set up to be tricked by their own sloppiness.

Because we agree to remember the Order of the Black Sheep are easily fooled by the absurdly, obviously obvious.

Whew! – thank you for sticking with me. I'm obviously almost, nearly done.

One last thing before you go – there's one tiny perspective spinning in real slow.

Since we are agreeable to referring to the *not-obvious-yet* – as the unconscious somewhere, the noys must <u>already</u> be there.

> *Wait, let's paws with these words.*
> says Kiva.

Since it's **in the** unconscious, it must already be there.

THE GAME IS CHANGE

"*What has to be there*," you might say.

It has to be somewhere, right?!

I mean something could not be unconscious if it wasn't conscious, before a time we can remember.

Perhaps, we have been here all along.

What if we agreed to remember an awareness beyond the embers – a distinct, very faint, cloud of candy cotton, of a recognition we have long since forgotten?

Is it possible,

I am remembering what once was lost in the dark,

when I forgot about Magic in the Amusement Park?

Is it possible I can remember Magic, while I play,

So I can remember how perfectly perfect,

I am set up today?

Is it possible, we discarded artifacts along the way to help us re-find our amusing trail? An absolutely unavoidable pathway of forgetting our magic and riding our roller coaster cars off the rail?

And then, we even forgot that we were lost, and the cards we were playing with were tossed.

And that's a positive thing, right?

When our roller coaster cars jump off the predictable and obvious scale, we become open to the possibility of magic and find our way back to the Amusement Park trail.

AMUSEMENT PARK

Let's agree to agree:

We ate too much candy and we had too much sex. We drank too much wine, gambled in the casino, and divided up the rest. We stepped on others in our foolish pursuits and then proceeded to throw up in our roosts.

Then we judged it and ridiculed it – and then we gave it a name. All the while we did it, we called it a game. And despite the attempt to have a little fun, we simply could not un-be with what we'd just done.

We did not notice in our stupor, the slinging of blame was making us stupider. We did not notice we were covering ourselves *in visible* shame and making a mask that hid our true character's name.

We thought we could enjoy playing with naughtiness, while masking ourselves with the not so obvious. And then we un-remembered, and then we forgot – for it was far easier than sitting with the pain of our thoughts.

And this is how we each cast a spell upon ourselves. We tripped and fell over the *not-obvious-yet*; got caught up in something we never were going to do – which felt so overpowering, we locked it away for later stew.

And we've been doing it over and over, in lifetime after lifetime again – leaving unimaginable things behind with invisible chagrin. Broken hearts, distorted memories and indignant speak. Then the doubt crept in and we became weak.

What was once sacred soon became dull and dark. We started building castles made of sand and then we forgot about the Amusement Park.

Now we see the discourse and we see the erosion. Now our drink bottles end up in the ocean. Hard to know what we are feeling, hard to know what to do — when the thing we love so much is covered in poo.

Thankfully, enduring the savage concourses of colonizing men — the elders and shamans kept the secrets for us when. Someone remembered a group they could trust: *The Order of the Black Sheep*.... **Wait... that's us!**

So I am trusting you and only you — when you are in the Amusement Park you practice compassion until you are amused. I feel you get the seriousness of my intent. It's not to restrict or inhibit you, that's not what I meant.

It's to guide you away from covert deceptions — to maximize your joy and minimize your lessons. So from this moment forward the power of addictions no longer have the power of a *not-obvious-yet* affliction.

Yes, to all this, I agree to agree!

Instead of the ways, of customary seeing; let's become agreeable in the ways of, comfortably being. We now all, agree to agree, to evolve with grace and ease. And, that it is indeed a privilege, to be of the black sheep breed.

We agree to agree therefore, to feel the *not-obvious-yet* pain in ways we never have before. We agree to agree to be so efficient with the flow, we can easily and instantly let the *not-obvious-yet* and *obvious* go.

AMUSEMENT PARK

And as we learn non-resistance and ride the Arc, we each together co-create the Amusement Park.

Now-here (actually on the next page) come those words again of the **4 Signs** rhyme.

Will I allow myself now, to feel the column of Light?
Am I agreeable now, to feel the excitement inside?

Am I now, big enough, to make alchemy ecstatic?
Am I really, open to the Possibility of Magic?

Am I agreeable to not build too small?
Can I help build an Amusement Park for All?

𝓐

Now

With These

4 Signs I've Become

Agreeable. I Am Aware,

Alert, Awake, and I Am Ample.

So with Willingness, I now embark.

I Am Slowing Down, and I Am Agreeably

Agreeable Inside the Amusement Park. I Am

Communicating with Precision, Allowing a

Compassionate Agreeability to Flower

As I Remember,

I Am, That I Am;

My Light & Power.

I Say Yes to My Heart

So I take it you had a new experience with this lexicon. I trust your magic. Put the Ace in your Pass Port, and let's move on.

AMUSEMENT PARK

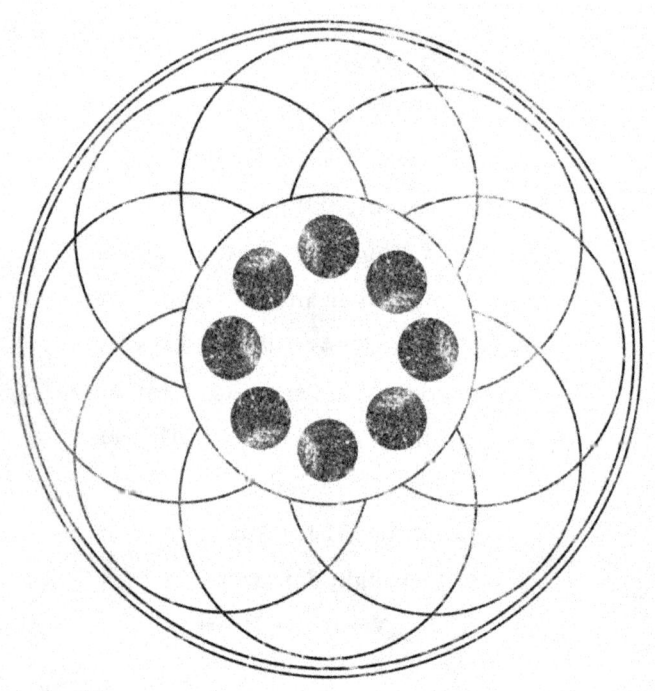

Page 92 - I Am Agreeable

ACT I:

Portal of Entry

Scene Four: *Use Imagination*

It took some time to lay out our play and I appreciate you listening in a new kind of way.

So here you are in the blackness before you. You have been walking up the trail and have come to a place where the terrain seems to be directing you into a narrow forested area to explore – it's hard to tell… there seems to be a great overgrown wooden entry door.

AMUSEMENT PARK

You stand at what looks to be the entrance to the show. Everything in you feels ready to go.

You have agreed to be agreeable in the Amusement Park play.

You have deepened your commitment in yourself today.

And as you are sincere with your intent, the Amusement Park has taken notice and is formulating in assent. For AP4 is as agreeable as you are agreeable – with it.

You have a light on your head and a wag in your tail – because the mystery is magic and today you set sail.

The Intelligence has given us what It created with godly affection:

An Amusement Park of Divine Perfection.

Ah yes, you are re-remembering now.

Be agreeable, so you can find and board Noah's Arc.

Once on Noah's ride, amused you are and free to bark.

Imagine Amusement Park solves any difficult dog dishes.

Imagine Amusement Park grants any true dog heart's wishes.

Imagine the journey in Amusement Park is easy and peaceful, so long as you are agreeable.

Now in the Amusement Park there is a collective to look for; it's your responsibility to ask for help from other Amusers galore. Because that is the one thing that sets us apart – from other magicians who forget about the Park. We agree to agree that we notice the moment we start to forget. And precisely in that moment, assistance we get.

We agree to agree that when shame creeps in and we withdraw, a process is activated in our community for the healing of all. We agree to remember and become shame free today, because we are emerging from a previously obviously obvious, ordinarily ordinary, agreed-upon play.

For we have already agreed to agree that obvious magic does not work in the Park – except to lead us back into the *not-obvious-yet* to re-embark.

We are in agreement then, that we are simply learning – and by embracing this we evolve by ease and grace returning.

Haven't we?

For we now see when we engage with these older kinds of magic, we start to un-remember the Amusement Park.

This is why so many magicians in the Obvious Realm are confused. They can feel what they know to be true – and cannot remain amused.

It is therefore our responsibility to build Amusement Park.

And to that, we are all agreeable, in bark.

AMUSEMENT PARK

We are moving to a backwards in time.

Our breath has run out and now we are all blue.

Now, the time piece suspended, before our very eyes.

For in a moment, the pendulum swings through.

Traveling soon off to distant shore.

We go back

into

the now future.

Noah's Arc again, we shall find inside.

Someone wrote about it long ago, we now know,

So that we'd find it when we were ready to butter-fly.

Appearing when we are totally non-resistant.

The Absolutely Agreeable Assistant.

Do you yet, get it?

AP4 Now

Yes.

So do you get it? Or are you confused?

Kiva says:

Confusion is Prerequisite to Becoming Amused.

Before we forgot our magic, we were on Noah's Arc so nicely unbruised – wondering what it was like to be *totally* Amused.

Before the Park we were in a heavenly vignette. And we couldn't as angels see, the *not-obvious-yet*. That we had to start in a most ordinary of fashion to fully appreciate the gifts, of all of creation.

So the Intelligence gave us the plans for the AP4 garden, to build for the entire cosmos to receive a pardon. We agreed to remember that we carried the plans in our imagination, and to share and build them on this earthly space station.

It was in simple ignorance that we landed on dry land. Remember, when we started building castles made of sand?

And we had to, remember?

The Earth was quite dangerous. We found caves and fire – and safety did surface. We stared for hours into the coals, which kept us warm and cooked our bowls.

Then someone got jealous and someone got cold. Remember when no one lived, to be very old?

And that is where we started from after we forgot. Because we had to – we were all so overwrought. We built the Ordinary Realm first and obviously, it hurt. And, since us angels weren't accustomed to building in ordinary ways – as soon as we became humans, we lived ordinary malaise.

We made the agreement, yes we did – which turned the life of an angel upon its head.

The agreement to which we all agreed: to create Amusement Park, to remember we could be amused by balancing the positive and negative – and completing the Arc.

So the Master sent us out on an Arc of His shower, requiring the Feminine Earth to balance His Masculine power. Noah's Arc we rode - until an agreeable couple, sprung our Flower.

We chose this lifetime and our unfolding – and to be at peace with it, we are now beholding. To this, we are agreeable.

Noah's Arc is suddenly crossable, and now **Anything is Possible.**

So to summarize the entire introduction into one simple equation: You said **Yes** to your Heart, and therefore all of creation. So, we agree to agree to carry this first agreement on from the start:

We Always Say Yes to Our Heart.

And we'll agree to at least eight more for all of humanity in the journey beyond – because by reading further, we've agreed to agree with what the Amusement Park spawns.

Now, one last hint, before you land in the park. When you find someone seemingly against you and dark.

Turn the truth around to see the obvious door – that they too have forgotten they are lost, in AP4.

THE GAME IS CHANGE

Congratulations,

You've just ridden the **Shame Blaster!**

Hurry up, for there's no way to go faster.

You've just ridden a vortex right into Act Two.

Kiva, just maybe, lets you out of her doggie day-care zoo. Until on Noah's Arc you fly away, making your life more like puppy's play.

Check your pockets – and what do you find? The Amusement Park has **32 tokens** to you assigned. One for each of the $8 in quarters with which you started – a reward for traveling the path uncharted.

There are 5 Amusement Park rides to come:

The first ride, **Hall of Mirrors**, requires just one token. It is quite persistent (believe me, I'm not joking;)

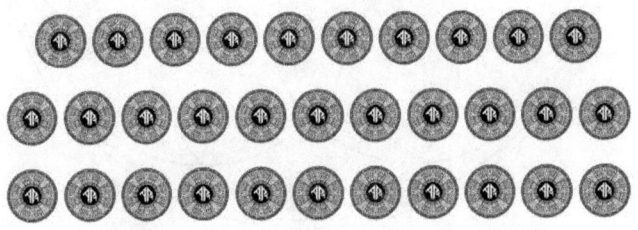

The remaining rides, cost double each time — to challenge you to keep up with our play and ongoing rhyme.

5 more rides, and you are out.

I Am Agreeable - Page 99

AMUSEMENT PARK

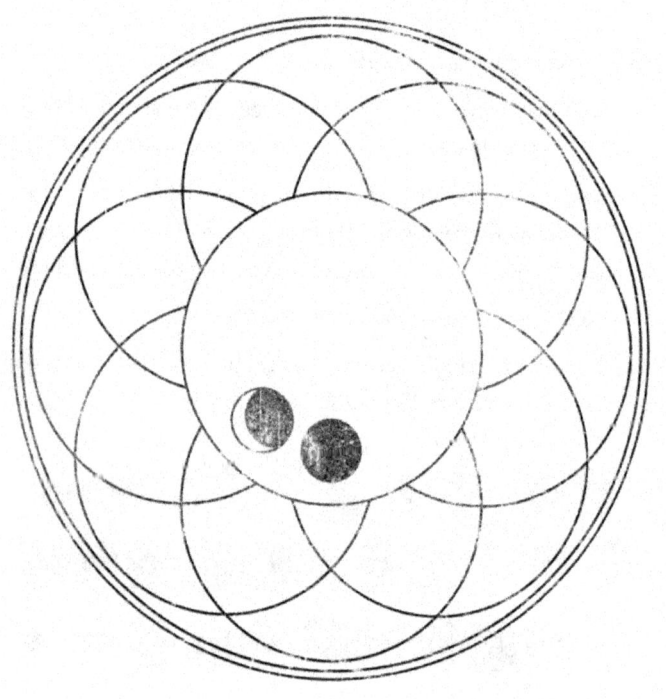

Act II

Hall of Mirrors

Scene One:

Oh Shit, I said Yes! Now What?

Above the horizon you catch a glimpse of the waxing moon. A crescent of light on the side of a great darkened balloon.

Now you are noticing you are slightly rising and spinning. The Shame Blaster has left you feeling quite a bit dizzy. You are realizing you have arrived somewhere new – came right up on a giant holographic corkscrew. So here you are standing all alone, in a great big cavern so far from home.

The only light is between your eyes. It points in the direction you recognize. There is dense mist hanging in the air. For this, how could you possibly prepare? Everything is damp and chilling to your bones.

Wait a minute! Where are my clothes?

You now wear simple sandals, with a simple cloak.

You left the Shame Blaster and kept the Ace of Spades as intent.

You're in agreement by reading farther, you given your consent.

And you won't read too fast and you won't skip ahead – for reading with agreeability bakes magical bread.

We agreed to agree that once you enter Amusement Park, you are agreeable to this prose, until you ride Noah's Arc.

As the memory of the Shame Blaster fades, you come to terms with what is next. What are you noticing? Perhaps you feel – *perplexed*?

Above you there is nothing but an abyss that is dark.

You wonder, "Is this really the… Amusement Park?" Below you is solid ground, flat with some sand. You still have your passport in hand. Ahead, you are pointing the light with your eyes. Wait, is that another sign, you spy?

It's hard to read here from this stationary place. A few steps closer, perhaps you can take. Only a few though, as the trail might disappear. The darkness may swallow your path, you fear.

Approaching the sign, it becomes increasingly clear.

I am inside some great round courtyard here.

How

Am

I

Keeping Score

With My

Self

?

You say under your breath.

> *How am I keeping score with myself?*

You notice this one is pointing the other way around. Does this mean you go back, or perhaps you go down?

The sign is affixed to a stone wall going up into the abyss. Your hands must touch it – smooth and hard to dismiss. As your fingers explore the walls for imperfection, you walk alongside giving your surroundings an inspection.

You notice the more you continue around, there is nothing here except loose sand on solid ground. So with one hand touching the vertical wall, you explore with your headlamp, the scope of the hall.

There are no doorways, windows or even any beams. Could anyone hear your screams? It's like being in a great stone cup –

where the only way out, is impossibly up.

Oh, another sign just up there. Perhaps an answer to your prayer.

Oh, wait. That's the very same one. Where you have started, you have now only just begun.

How many times have you done *this* before? Wandered back to here again, once, twice… maybe more. As you sit and ponder your annoying situational dance. A thought comes to you…

This isn't by chance.

This is a cosmic soul reunion rendezvous.
Where the only way out, is through.

You suddenly wonder.

"Hey. Where *did* you and Supertramp, get along to?"

Aw, I am so glad you asked.

I'll agree to entertain your distracted mind for a moment or two. But only to amuse your senses, and help you follow through.

Just before we left the Sky Temple, Supertramp and I agreed to agree that our gifts would spring out for all to see. And that's exactly what happened – so earnestly.

First he spent a week in a hotel, and I in the countryside, while things coalesced for our River House ride. I started landscaping for the upcoming rent and joyful time by myself was spent – making backyards beautiful and imaging new things to invent.

THE GAME IS CHANGE

One day in a plot while musing a jest, a honey bee buzzed by just off my breast. And then a voice spoke from a nearby sparkling white flower. I paused and heard in a commanding love shower:

> *Start a mystery school at the River House.*
> *Your name on the end – E you will fashion.*
> *A MysterE School of Communal Alchemy,*
> *Conscious Enterprise & Evolutionary Compassion.*

And before it had started, it had already begun. For I could not, un-hear those words. And I knew somewhere, somehow, it was already done. This scariest of directives couldn't be simply dismissed. It came to me in a moment, of gardening bliss.

And then I sat with the reality of my play. I had $8 in quarters, with more coming on Friday.

Now my mind is a little like yours – easily beckoned and often confused; for this decree came in a package which left me completely amused.

Regardless; here I was unbelievably alone, typing those words into my incredibly smart phone. Landscaping in an ordinary client's backyard had mysteriously given me, a new deck of playing cards.

"I don't even know what a mystery school is," I said – to the voice as it disappeared in an unturned bed; leaving me unaided with a very ordinary task at hand. Musing I went on, thrusting my shovel into the land.

Something about this experience absolutely did muster – for a spirit in me had quite the new luster. And that's what I preceded to follow and do – step into fields that were completely new.

AMUSEMENT PARK

I was about to move back into the River House, with my children and mother (no longer my spouse). And now, who me, start a MysterE School? This feels like a deep and dangerous water whirlpool.

And, that exactly where you now stand; like me, you have manifested a similarly mysterious land.

You might be curious: How do I follow through with this new vibration, of making agreements with an amusing narration?

That however, is for you to digest. It's important to guide you back to your vision quest – now that a few steps, you have progressed.

I bring you back clearly before the last signpost – reminding you of your agreements with our AP4 host.

And I know that you know:

As you continue your AP4 trek,
the more agreeable with magic, you get.

How
Am
I
Keeping Score
With My
Self
?

THE GAME IS CHANGE

Wait, this sign is pointing the other way round.
Does that mean I go back, or somehow go down?

In the perplexity, I turn in the other direction.
For something is shimmering for my inspection.

Noys I didn't quite notice before;
A sparkling on the ground impossible to ignore.

I walk back and crouch where I once did stand,
A map of sorts is barely visible, down in the sand.

It is about the length of my arms outstretched.
Crudely available and precisely sketched.

With both of my hands, I brush aside the grain.
My headlamp reveals lines sculpted in the terrain.

Etched into the stone from an earlier now,
What does this diagram, to me endow?

Pressing my fingers into the contours and lines,
I think, *This must be a map of an ancient kind.*

AMUSEMENT PARK

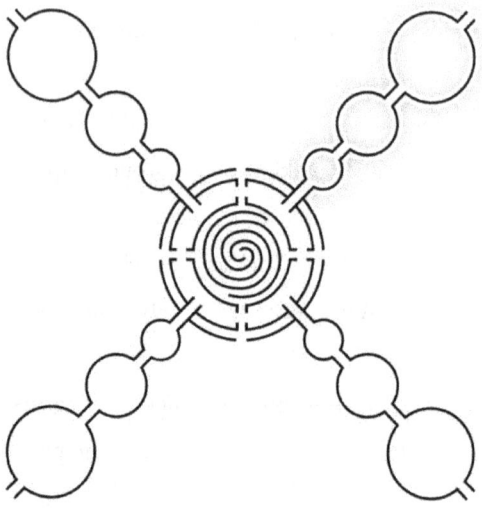

One of the chart's wings is brighter than the rest.
It seems to be guiding me toward the sign as a test.

THE GAME IS CHANGE

You stand up and turn to the sign you were just noticing – something is new there; it looks like an opening.

Suddenly the map on which you are standing, groans and shakes under your feet and begins expanding. In fact the diagram is rising by itself to a hover, as a slab of rock above the ground to cover.

Actually, no. Wait!

Now, where has the ground gone? This is some kind of strange otherworldly, phenomenon. Slowly and with ease, the map elevates under your feet and becomes a moving walkway street. Except you can't step in any direction at all – for where there was earth before, is now a great fall. You are unsteady and wobbly for a bit, as your balance gets adjusted to the new movement.

> But, wait a second! Strangely enough, I am **not** moving!
> And now the sign is coming toward me – so confusing.
>
> Am I in a kind of holographic representation,
> Of everything approaching me, in divine orchestration?

Looking above, you see familiar constellations. Underneath however are those only seen on vacation.

Turning back toward the advancing scene, the curved walls are moving like a giant movie screen. Below the sign is a narrow doorway of stone. You know that's your entrance to the next amusement zone.

So you steady yourself as an undersized door, arrives in the side of a great moving stone goblet to explore.

> *I guess, I'm going to find out how I keep score.*

AMUSEMENT PARK

To get through the passage you must bow, and then erect yourself back to standing somehow. There is nothing here that you can view. So you keep still until you pass this place or know what to do.

Another wall and another door is approaching right quick. Your reflexes are important for the stone is pretty thick. So strange to not be moving at all while things flow past. Is there a way to slow it down, or make it go fast?

Things are simply happening on their own accord. Impossible to predict, and not possible to be bored. Into another emptiness, followed by another opening in stone – you can only breathe with your fears, for now you are simply alone.

"That's three doorways I have passed through," you observe; tracing the map with your fingers alongside the curves. "I must be out here on the furthest round juncture, of this great labyrinth kind of stone structure."

Now you notice, things are not moving like they were before. You trust now, you won't be smashed by a moving wall or door.

You train your head beam ahead of your sight. There seems to be a spectacle of extraordinary delight.

No angular lines. Everything is rounded and covered in glass. Only legions of mirrored facets staring back at you, en masse.

Like landing in an inside-out disco ball – you are still, alone and hovering, in a great circular hall.

The only thing to do is to be calm and present here – as you find yourself the center, of a looking glass sphere.

THE GAME IS CHANGE

You know this is a place to notice and paws. And who couldn't with mirrors looking back, just because. The reflections are above, around and even beneath. They are in every direction — so you'd better just breathe.

No matter where you point your light, the reflection is the same. It's you, playing you, in the Amusement Park game. Yes, you've brought yourself here.

Remember?

What have you left yourself, from way up ahead?
What agreements were made, and what have you said?
Only your mind could make up an obvious threat.
Can you remember to illuminate, the *not-obvious-yet?*

Oh right, I can make this reflection sparkle!
I can set an intent, and then take it much farther.

I feel the excitement inside, and a column of light around,
So I steady my feet to the ground.

In my passport, is my very first card.
I remember the words. They are:

A

Now

With These

4 Signs I've Become

Agreeable. I Am Aware,

Alert, Awake, and I Am Ample.

So with Willingness, I now embark.

I Am Slowing Down, and I Am Agreeably

Agreeable Inside the Amusement Park. I Am

Communicating with Precision, Allowing a

Compassionate Agreeability to Flower

As I Remember,

I Am, That I Am;

My Light & Power.

I Say Yes to My Heart

THE GAME IS CHANGE

With this incantation your headlamp gets dimmer. Above you to the right, a reflection starts to shimmer. The words are bright and impossible to ignore. It's even possible, you've seen them before.

There is no way out of this amusing animation, for one day you too, will exist only in narration. But for now, this reflection has adorned you in a red top hat. With gold starry letters spelling out: ***"I Am That!"***

Now other images are appearing right, left, up and down. Facets moving like a Rubik's Cube turning a round. More reflections in your universe sparkle to life. Meanwhile music surrounds the scene of a fool playing fife.

Each image shifts, turns and corrects its course – until it's before you by way of centrifugal force. In each reflection, an old video for your contemplation. For there you are again, in all past compromising situations.

"Oh wow, I'd forgotten I had been there... And said that to him. Did I really? Oh wow, Yep, me too. That's incredibly grim."

Except that in every reflection, you are wearing that red top hat – which by the way, with gold starry letters reads: ***I Am That!***

Scenes are playing over and over – again and again, as the mirrored tiles bring more and more memories in. You are playing along with old friends and some others, making amends and exploring your druthers.

Some you recognize and some you sort of do. You wonder, "Are these reflections of my past lives too?" With a continual hum of methodical clicking and clacking, the puzzle keeps entertaining with constant re-manufacturing.

You are not in control and most certainly 100% responsible, for all the feelings you feel are not always comical. And as this play continues to spin around impressing, it starts to become well, slightly overwhelming.

Now, an awareness in you is starting to bloom,

How can I play with this puzzle, and get out of this room?

Perhaps there's another way I can be – this instance.
I know! I can open my heart, and simply play witness.

As soon as you notice the twist of this performance, the tiles become responsive and lessen their swarming. With a blink and a nod and the acknowledgement of your heart, each tile slows down and takes its place, in a mosaic of art.

It's now becoming apparent to you once more, as you stand here with no ceiling and no floor.

The more responsible and amused I become with this play,
The lighter my heart feels, and I can soon be on my way.

Now the images are sparkling, spinning and sorting themselves, until they are like millions of book covers, sitting on shelves.

"How do I want to leave this room?" is what you want to know. So AP4 responds to your intent, with one last show.

Like Vanna White turning tiles in front of her crowd, the Wheel of Fortune reveals what's behind its own cloud. A line of mirrors one by one turn themselves around quite artfully:

BLESS WHATEVER YOU SEE

AND USE LANGUAGE IN HARMONY

With your awareness you look beyond the letters, and see beyond your misperceptions and imagined errors. And as the round stone tablet under your sandals begins to hum, it's apparent, the room is moving back to where you came from.

Crouching down so as to avoid the low door frame, you turn back to face the inside out disco ball video game. And what can you now so plainly see with perspective?

My life is a beautiful collective, and is always self-selected.

With this truth you have certainly agreed for the Amusement Park has set you free.

As you feel the wind of the moving door around your frame. You stay crouched and turn to face the very next play. "It's dark again," you say, feeling you were here just prior – now becoming more comfortable with being a high flyer.

With your hands and light you trace the map at your feet. You say: "I must now be in the middle chamber of this wing. What is its magic? Do I dare even speak?"

Instead of looking at the card in your passport, you simply remember the feeling of your intent. Suddenly the room begins sparkling with some new event. It's the same and half the size, somehow, as you view it with curiosity that allows. The tiles are exactly as you left them in the last room. What are you here to witness and to exhume?

And with this awareness, the images activate increasing in size and focused on faces. This goes on until there is nothing in view, except every person you have known to be you.

Millions of faces now staring back at you with their eyes. Some bright and shiny, others in disguise. Some in fear, others in a more obvious pride. Some are blank, while others trying to look away.

Do you ever remember feeling this way?

Yes, I Am That!

This declarative acceptance of your *not-obvious-yet* situation is giving you the sensation of – *I can do this*, elation.

"What are these faces inviting me to see?" you inquire. Are you inspired to take the scene much higher?

With this budding confidence something else does fashion. A growing feeling of universal self-compassion. For you see on this journey of life, everyone does the best they can with strife.

So you generate the feeling of love deep from within, and share it from your eyes with your identical twins. The mirrored mosaic responds to your feeling, to magnify their focus only on seeing.

Every set of eyes from every single face, are now on each reflective tile. This becomes all you can see for this one little while. Millions of sets of human eyes suddenly looking at you. You stand, and slowly turn to take them in, as review.

Blue, brown, grey, beady and bright. A few are really green even in this low light. The eyes change colors, although the pairs linger. It's a dancing, flashing matrix of visionary winkers.

And what happens when you wink in the game? The eyes wink back at you and then become the same – until you are looking into millions of your own eyes...

Everyone is me, I summarize.

"How do I want leave this room?" is what you want to know.

So the Amusement Park responds to your intent with one last show. Like Vanna White turning tiles in front of her crowd, the Wheel of Fortune reveals what's behind its own cloud.

ACCEPTANCE OF HUMANESS

LIGHTENS YOUR LOAD

The map under your sandals begins to hum. The room is moving back again to where you came from. With this truth you have certainly agreed, for the Amusement Park has set you free.

Crouching down so as to avoid the low frame, you feel the wind and turn to face the very next play. There's no need to look at the diagram under your feet, for you know you are entering the next and nearest chamber suite.

The play is happening more efficiently now, and with more speed. Hesitation and doubt have left, as you have, agreed to agree.

The feeling you are carrying in your heart – seems to have landed here before the start. For the chamber is already activating its mirrors. It likes you are embodying, the AP4 triggers.

This chamber is certainly much smaller, and the tiles are much larger. There, on each of the reflective rotating screens, are images of you standing here, in simple means.

You see the sandals and the tunic threads. Now the red top hat appears again on all of your heads. Your faces shimmer and there are canes in your hands. The message is clear, *I Am That* on all your headbands.

Now all the mirrors flip upside down and reverse but one. You're choosing to watch, what is soon to be undone.

It's a play of two people with one in control. The other's a victim of being stuck in a hole. Each is pointing fingers at the other – looking like a feud between a son and a brother. "Their faces appear the same – wait that's me! How could this possibly be something to see?"

Your curious nature is sensed by the Amusement Park hall. The mirrors turn back and right side up, and then re-install. One by one, the reflections reveal videos of antiquated plays. It's you in the past, in older ways.

Always one bigger, or smarter, or luckier, or stronger. Always one crying over spilled milk and lost toys much longer. You feel your anger as you watch your earlier drama – of someone else getting their ways and causing more trauma.

Finally, your heart ever-so-slightly starts to burn and pop.

Hey! I know how to make this madness stop!

> *I created that, and that, and — oh, every time,*
> *Right about the moment, I forgot to speak in rhyme.*

> *I took the play of life as much too threatening,*
> *And I constructed evidence, to create that reckoning.*

> *I did it for my learning, I remember now and see!*
> ***I Am That!*** *And with this truth, I am free.*

Every acknowledgment diminishes the clicking and clacking. Then the mirrored room becomes less than a silent spattering. Each mirror returns to reflect carbon prints of your eyes. And each set of you sends out a beam of light, which supplies your heart with a feeling of radical allowance.

It's one of astounding self-reliance.

Sensing completion, you trace a finger along the map lines, and the stone tablet under your sandals begins to whine. You now know, the small door approaches you from behind.

Looking up at the receding tidal vision, you bend down to see the Wheel of Fortune letters, turning around. The letters one by one reveal what's in the AP4 vault:

EVERYONE IS RESPONSIBLE

AND NO ONE IS AT FAULT.

AMUSEMENT PARK

And to this you most certainly have agreed to agree, for the Amusement Park room just set you free.

Turning toward the oncoming wall, make sure you have made yourself, not too tall.

The scene shifts back to the courtyard of the great stone cup. There is no way out, again, except to go up.

The map becomes again, a part of the floor. And you are free to roam around the chamber once more. The door through which you just came, has melted into the flawless walls of this domain.

However your little trek seems to have left the old sign looking a bit funny – for the ways you keep score now, are far more sunny.

Walking over to the sign and giving it a spin, you're amazed at what happens then – the sign reorganizes the letters and clicks and pops; and then suddenly, its bottom becomes its top.

I

Am

Speaking

Heart Language: For

Every

Word

Is a

Prayer.

And to this you most certainly agree to agree, for you have seen the power of intent, and felt your heart's acknowledgement.

No longer will you use the language of the ordinary, to explain the old agreements made; when there is awareness of compassion for all, in the human parade.

There is certainly more to explore in this great stone cup, where the only way out is through, and the impossible is up.

You are wise enough at this here junction, to know that the map in the center has an extraordinary function. "There are three more wings of three to explore," you muse…

I am more efficient now, I choose.

I imagine myself going through the labyrinth with ease.
To this, I can most certainly agree to agree.

So I go back to the center and with my hands once anew –
Move the sand outward to expand my growing world view.

This time, to the slight dismay of my expectation,
There's another symbol here for my curious flirtation.

The eyes I just left in that room,
Seem to have followed me with something of a clue.

AMUSEMENT PARK

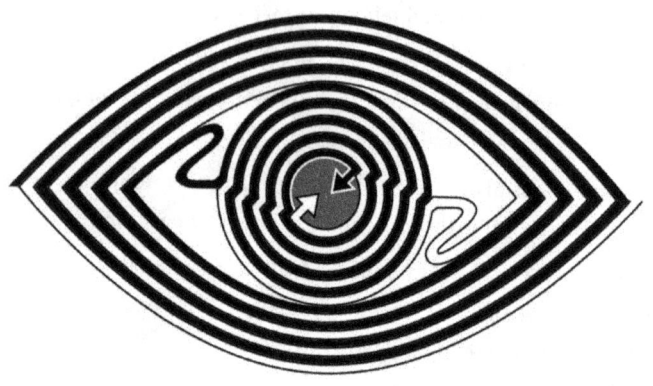

Isn't this interesting?

>Two arrows; one white and one black point into the eye.
>From which two grooved pathways lead, out to the sides.

You have a sudden curiosity,

>*Does my passport have the answer?*
>*It would be great at this moment, to have an enhancer.*

Fortunately, your passport explains the clue. Indeed, the next page, has the answer for you.

The Eye of Truth
Labyrinth of Innocence.

Hold your pointer fingers pointed to the sky.

My left is my Mother & my right is my Father.

It doesn't matter if you've never met,
or if they're long distance, or not even in flesh.

Your enmeshment created my humanness.

Trace your fingers from each outside
corner, left & right, one dark & one light.

I honor your individual journeys that brought
Both of you together for my conception.

Trace your fingers to the center.

You gave me my life in this momentary discretion.
Since then, I've brought lots of stupid shit to confession.

I am sorry and I know better now. I was learning.
I did all these things to wake myself up.
And I am grateful now. Thank you for my life.

I forgive you — and then I am forgiven.

As soon as your fingers lift off of the Eye of Truth inscription, the stone begins to hum and the sand dances in encryption. Once more the floor is covered in grit. And what's below is a mystery now, you'll have to admit.

So you kneel down at the center, and with your hands once again, spread the sand outward, with a child-like innocent grin. This time, to the slight elation of your admiration, the other symbol is back for your re-examination.

Now the wing 180° from the last explored is lighted – as the one to go toward. Standing up, you look in the map's illuminated route, and on the far wall another sign you make out.

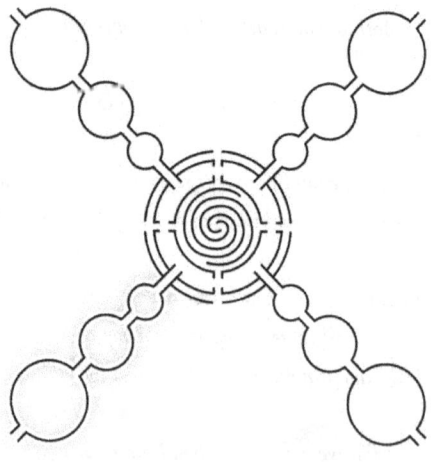

THE GAME IS CHANGE

Suddenly the map on which you are standing, groans and shakes under your feet and begins expanding.

In fact the diagram is rising by itself, to a hover. A slab of rock inches above the ground, you cover. The floor gives way and the walls begin to carriage. A narrow doorway appears behind the sign to the next passage.

Crouching now, you read the sign. It's pretty straight.

What Am I Ready to Remove From My Plate?

AMUSEMENT PARK

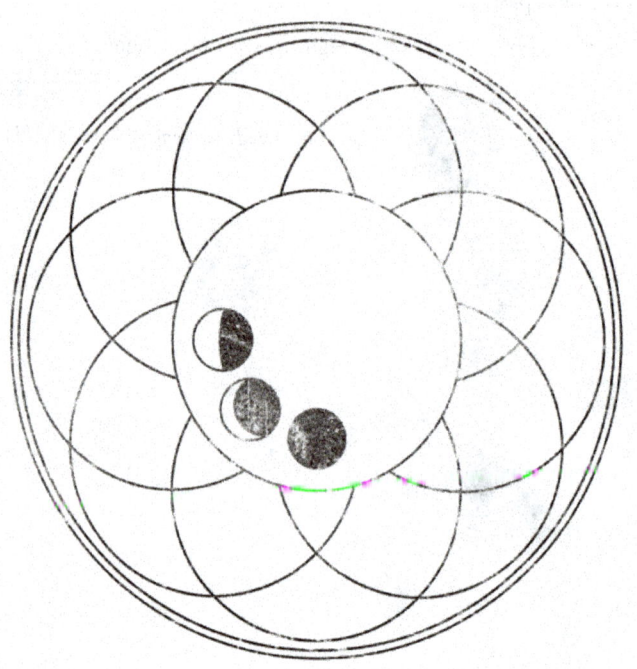

Page 126 - I Am Agreeable

Act II

Hall of Mirrors

Scene Two:

Where Are My Hands?

Above, in the night sky, you catch a glimpse of the first quarter moon; half-light on one side of the great darkened balloon. You steady yourself as it arrives — another undersized door — in the side of a moving stone goblet to explore. Through this door you calculate.

I guess, I am going to clean my plate.

What

Am

I

Ready to Remove

From My

Plate

?

To get through the passage you bow. And to flow with the ride, you vow.

Now you've found yourself in the next chamber glassed; the same dimensions and mirrors, of the last.

Like landing in again, an inside-out disco ball – you are still alone, and hovering in a circular hall. The only thing to do is to be absolutely calm and present here – as you find yourself the center of a familiar glass sphere.

Except here, in the mirrors all around are empty reflections. Looking at your surroundings, you notice you aren't in any direction. How strange to be looking into mirrors with no one there. You move right, left, and wave. No one sees your stare.

You squint with your eyes as the light here is slimmer. The more you look for yourself, the more it goes dimmer. You say, "What is the magic of this small, inside-out, mirrored ball? I'm not sure of anything right now – nothing at all."

It is beginning to dawn on you – you are terribly alone. There is no one here at all, only endless looking glass and stone.

The headlamp is on, you figure, from looking at your feet. It can't be seen in the mirrors though; how bittersweet. Why isn't the magic of this room revealing? It feels a whole lot like the all too familiar, glass ceiling.

Remembering your passport, you sound out incantations. Nothing happens however, leaving you only with resignation. The words you speak, are but echoes in this chamber. What is the key to activating this room to become a savior?

The more you try making something transpire – the more the darkness reveals you as the lone occupier. Something in you feels like a way you have before. Locked in a glass room and no way to find the door.

For what happens when you find yourself in such a situation? Do you fall down into frustration? Silence is the weight of your circular repeating situation. It keeps pressing in on you, like an inverted invisible foundation.

Looking down at the diagram, you trace repeatedly with your digits – along the lines, exploring all potential hidden limits. Your headlamp flickers and fades into the darkness. Now you are left here alone and kneeling without harness. Hopelessness arrives in your imagined predicament. What is the use of this ridiculous invisible instrument?

For in such times of self-imposed hindrance;

> *The only thing I can do, is ask, for Divine assistance.*

You abruptly stand without concern for falling – with no more interest in extending your self-imposed, poor-me stalling.

> *Hey God, whoever you are - I require a bit of grace.*
> *Can you lend a hand with how to clear my plate?*

In your soles you feel something start to hum. The room comes to life with the heartbeat of your drum. As the images around you brighten to reveal, a multitude of poses of you in a kneel. Reflections of all the times in all your years, when you were all alone, and you finally found tears.

It's impossible to ignore: Every time you fell and wept before, someone was suddenly there, to open a door.

Then in each image on every single screen, is a familiar helper who quickly convenes. Lending you a hand to bring you from your knees – and relieving you from loads of misery.

Next to you in the red shiny hat, is Simple Simon; the gold letters on his band, keep on shinin'.

His face, of course, is a lot like yours – hard to forget and impossible to ignore. A little tune, he is singing with glee:

> *I am that, which I choose to be.*
> *I find it so strange, you look a lot like me.*
> *I am the warden and prisoner – who do you see?*

As your round stone disc broadens its vibration, the room is moving backward in a new graduation. You feel lighter and relieved of a conditional affliction – an old expiring conviction.

Crouching to avoid the oncoming structure, you turn ahead to face the new juncture. And what now, do you embody to believe?

Assistance always finds me, after I grieve.

With this truth you have certainly agreed, for the Amusement Park has set you free.

As you feel the wind of the moving door around you, you stay crouched to see what the next play gets into.

"It's dark again," you say, tracing the base of the grooved altar in the middle chamber. "I am asking for help this time, so not to falter."

The half-again larger room is sensing your cooperation, and begins responding to your self-important abdication. In this great hall, there are rows and rows of looking glass – making you the center of attention, in a simple mass.

In all the reflective tiles, there are people stretching on for miles. They look back at you with every emotion, from sadness to smiles.

The mirrors are re-sorting themselves with clicking and clacking. Until one tile is in front of you after tracking and stacking. Then, from the endless crowd, emerges the Man with the Red Hat. You know. The one with the brim saying, "***I Am That.***"

The mirror before you begins to expand and expand, until you are standing next to him on your hover stone stand. Sensing something simple, strange and profound; you drop to your knees, in the sand on the ground.

The Man in the Red Hat shouts:

"I see who you are, beyond all the shame. Are you ready to be clear, and proclaim?!"

Yes, I am transparent in all my thoughts and deeds,
For my gifts emerge, and to be in peace.

And with this absolute declaration, he reaches to a point under your chin. He then removes a façade from your face like an old snake's skin.

The Man in the Red Hat holds up the mask high for the multitudes to witness.

"Under this masquerade, I find nothing suspicious!"

And with this simple motion, things begin to spin into motion. The rock under you drones and whines, and the walls again move along their sacred lines. The room is moving outward once again, to a place you have not yet already been.

With this truth you have certainly agreed, for the Amusement Park has set you free.

Crouching down to avoid hitting your head, you look at the map of the oncoming stone bed.

You say, "I am entering the last of the rooms along this line; a completion of some perfect design. I'm sure I have this Amusement Park figured out now. This next room ought to be

THE GAME IS CHANGE

easier somehow."

And with this feeling of lightness and freedom, you let down your guard as you enter, the belly of a demon. For as suddenly as you are through the narrow aisle, you are surrounded by expansive truth to reconcile.

In this coliseum, the mirrors are extreme and bright, while the darkness around you is blacker than night. Immediately, you feel huge waves of being shaky and lost; like being on a sailboat, whose equilibrium has been tossed.

For how many times has *this* happened before? Right as you figured things out, you fell through a trapdoor. All angular lines now – sharp, pointy, and covered in glass. Only broken facets of mirrors, staring back at you en masse.

Like landing in a rotten inside-out old disco hall. You're alone and hovering, in a mis-shapen ball – the only thing is to be absolutely still and present here, finding yourself the center of a shattered looking glass sphere.

You see all those times when everyone got lost in their minds: "These things are fun," we summarized. We thought, "No one will ever know, but me. I have power over these things, you see. In fact, they are good for me, I truly feel. So just a little partaking with you, I will conceal."

Here in this once glittery hall, the party is over and the music plays on. You see someone sucking on a bottle, that's already gone. The floor is littered with empty cans, cigarette butts and discarded toys. Once the music sounded so good, but now it's just noise!

Someone's looking for dust at the edges of a mirrored table. Another is walking sideways, the best they are able.

A man in the shadows is chatting with young girls, while showering a computer monitor with pearls.

Over in the corner, a group of misguided women, so pretty. They are looking glamorous for the cameras of the supplying committee.

Another making plans to knock off her mother; to finance the purchase of just a little more buzzer.

Out in the open a woman twists and twirls, while the many men around her, play with her curls.

So strange that you can see what everyone is thinking – and in this moment, you haven't even been drinking.

Everyone is here, and yet they pretend they are isolated – wallowing in the mud and amusement they fabricated.

"This will be my last fix, of that, you can be assured. If he'll go home with me tonight, my life will be secured. I'll keep on eating donuts when I'm alone, and convince myself later, I sit on an unlucky throne. There's no way I can deal with the pain in my heart – so my doctor's prescription I'll take, as a innocent kick start.

For I'm always a moment away of controlling my habits – of taking my top hat off, and pulling out rabbits."

The reflections are above, around and even beneath. They are in every direction – so you'd better just breathe. No matter where you point your eyes, the reflection is the same. It's people playing people, in a not-so-amusing game. Yes it's you, them and us. We all placed ourselves on a similar bus.

So who is going to let you off the hooks hanging in this place? For comparison of yourself with others, never ever leads to grace.

That's what's happening in all these addicts' heads: "If I have more money, fame, or success – my addictions, I won't have to address.

So until such time as my life corrects itself and I get what I want,

I'll keep pretending not to notice, what's in the obvious."

Now remember what you left yourself, from way up ahead. What agreements were made, and what have you said?
Only your mind could make up an obvious threat.

> *What I am seeing is the obvious, there's no way to deny.*
> *The not-obvious-yet, must be higher in the sky.*

> *I really have no control over the madness in this orchestra pit.*
> *All I can do is leave it better than I found it.*

So you get out your broom and get keen with your observation. You get right to work cleaning up the mess in this room of damnation. You put things in the trash and get someone a quilt – straighten the furniture and hold someone crying to absolve their guilt. You whisper:

> *I'm sorry I participated, in our little mess.*
> *For these things now in me, I can address.*

> *For I Am That, and I am that, too,*
> *My persuasion only, a bit different than you.*

Looking back out to the reflections you see them all shift. The Man in the Red Hat is back.

Do you get the drift?
He sings…

> *Until you get things are simply, the way they are —*
> *You'll keep getting involved, and mess with your heart.*

> *And when you fully appreciate the entirety of the stage —*
> *You become inspired to spread your magic everywhere you play.*

And with this prayer, the stone plate under you cries – and the walls again move back along sacred lines. The room is moving backwards again, to the place you have already been.

With this you have certainly agreed, for the Amusement Park has set you free.

Crouching down so as to avoid the blow; three doorways through, you quickly flow. Back into the stone cup you thunder – this time, landing with wonder, for the stone map ceases not in its vibration. In fact, it has amplified.

Looking back from the way the walls did just move, you see the sign, which before beckoned you through.

> *Ha! What am I ready to remove from my plate?*

As you look to the post with sincere appreciation, the sign does a remixing of its posturing –

I

Am

Leaving It

Better Than I Found It,

4 Every

Scene

Is An

Offering.

And with that immediate emblematic rotation, the chamber moves to reveal, the next sign's location. And the walls before you spring into advance, as you read the words with more than a glance.

You see the sign approaching on the side of the rock bowl.

What am I ready to initiate that feeds my soul?

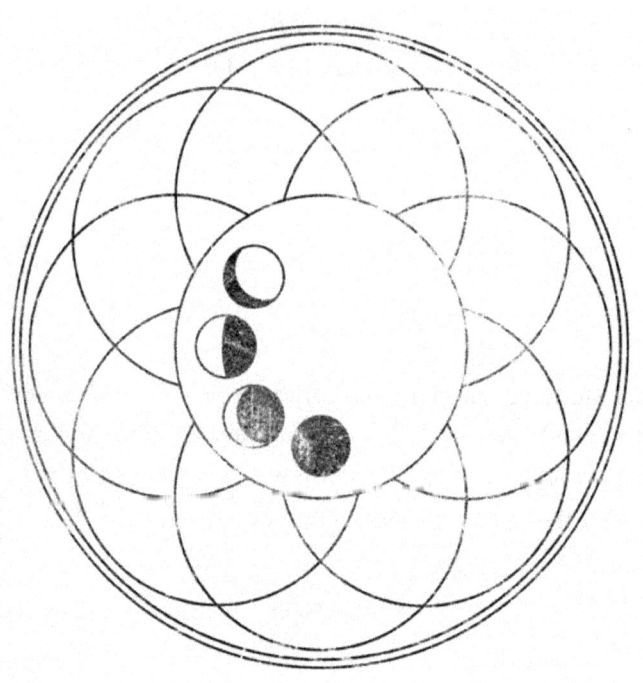

Act II

Hall of Mirrors

Scene Three:
Didn't See That Coming

Above in the sky you get glimpse of the waxing gibbous moon. It's mostly light, on the great darkened balloon.

So you steady yourself, as a door arrives in the side of the moving stone goblet – to explore as whole…

I am going to see about initiating my soul.

What

Am

I

Ready to Initiate

to Feed My

Soul

?

Once again surrounded by a chamber on the move, you look down as the ground falls away beneath your shoes. Noticing that the wing moving towards you is lighted, you bend down and trace your fingers on the circles united.

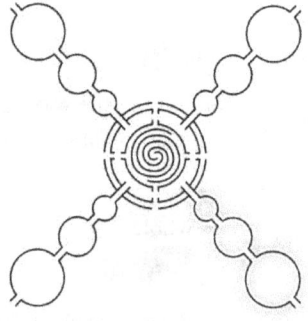

One room past and now another blows by; leaving you crouching in the third to demystify. You've completed seven stations of a symbolic cross – what's in store for you here, The Mythical Albatross?

For if the pattern repeats itself in this perpendicular fashion, you will complete a sign of universal, controversial compassion. You now see – that our mass human trickery crusade,

Begins by looking deeply and truthfully, at our own charades.

For what do you see mirrored back in the great hall of reflection? Millions of women who have been made, society's objectification.

As you point your head beam ahead of your sight, there seems to be a murmuring of extraordinary delight.

Everything here is bright, humming and covered in glass. Only facets of mirrors singing to you en masse.

Like landing in, an inside-out, refurbished disco ball – you are still, alone, and hovering, in an expansive circular musical hall.

The only thing to do is to be absolutely calm and present here, as you find yourself in the center of a singing glass sphere. You know this is a place to notice and paws.

And who couldn't with mirrors caroling back at you, just because.

The reflections are above, around and even beneath – as millions of women are walking toward you holding a wreath. From every direction in this glass compartment ocean – the women are marching and singing with devotion.

AMUSEMENT PARK

We've all played this silly game forever too long,
Won't you join us in our little freedom song?

We've danced on the sidelines and we've made ourselves available,
To agreements we should have known, were far too un-scalable.
We reinforced what was said about us amongst our friends,
We were acting complicit to our mutually agreed upon sins.

We've starred in your movies, and stood on your arms.
*Pretending not to notice, **we** placed ourselves in your harm.*
From this moment forward, we are holding out for men,
Who can gaze into our eyes and guide us to flower from within.

We offer you wreathes made of a sacred olive tree branch,
Representing our deep inner passions, we must advance.
When we feel safe enough in your true loving presence,
We give light to all kinds of new and fantastical events.

No longer will we hand over our hearts, to some little boy,
And no longer will we play with yours, like a toddler's toy.
We offer you the gift of everything this world can create,
With the promise of a better world, we can equally make.

And the song goes on as you are agreeable to the ballet, while the vibrations get louder with the chorus keeping up the wordplay.

THE GAME IS CHANGE

The new game we agree to play, has no clear cut winner.
No one is held back or ever called a sinner.
One where there is always a meal and a safe place to sleep,
One where we all get what we want, and good conversation to keep.

One where we stand as we are, with nothing to hide,
One where we own our humanness, and let go of our pride.
One impossible to lose ourselves, in a one card hand.
In this game, we agree to agree, to make promises stand.

You find yourself caught up in a dancing delirium, of imagining living in a perfect co-accountability aquarium. You look up to see half the reflections are now men – and with this awareness you continue to spin.

As the shindig goes on around and around, as the mass of humanity dances to the drums of sound. The stone tablet under your sandals begins to hum – the room is moving back to where you came from.

Crouching down so as to avoid the low door frame, you turn back to face the music hall video game.

And what can you now so plainly see today?

I am agreeable to relating in a new evolutionary way.

With this truth you have certainly agreed, for the Amusement Park has set you free.

As you feel the wind of the moving door around your frame, you stay crouched and turn to face, the very next play.

"It's dark again," feeling you were just here prior – "I am becoming more comfortable, with being a high flyer."

You trace the map around to where you belong; "I must be in this middle chamber now – what is its magic? Is there another song?"

With the curiosity of your intent, the room activates with an ensuing event. It's the same, and yet half the size somehow – as you view it with curiosity that allows. The tiles are moving and toward you still facing, only this time with smaller encasing.

Projected upon one mirror below and to the west, are football fans standing with hands on breast.

Now visible above your head and slightly behind, a second mirror shows a woman and baby standing on a corner with a sign. A third illuminates in front of where you are standing, to reveal a man getting a forearm branding. A fourth appears behind, so you turn to see the reflection; a political leader holding an electronic device, used for the election.

Each reflection is then brought to the front of your daydreaming - by the clicking and clacking of tiles, all moving and screaming.

The football fans are yelling, **You suck!**

The woman's sign reads, **Give a f*ck!**

The man's tattoo says, **She did it to me!**

The politician's screen blinks: **They are the ENEMY!**

Now the scenes come more quickly and the room begins to hum with the sound of millions of crying babies chewing sour gum. No one says a thing about the cheerleaders on the sidelines, or that ordinary people are using these same words to run our lives.

Now a quickening on the moving screens as the tiles turn and reshuffle. Infinite numbers of scenes are now viewable – illuminating angry communal scuffles.

It's impossible to see clearly any of the projections, for your senses are overwhelmed by their roaring dejections:

And the noise is ridiculously, and absurdly loud.

For who can hear above this noisy crowd?

Then all the mirrors go absolutely dark, in answer to your bark – and a deep voice calls out, and offers:

And now a word from our sponsors.

As the screens relight, they merge together into one large premier, one image stretched out over the entire inside of the sphere. You want to know, "How did they do that in here?"

Dominating the scene is an older bearded, debonair gentleman, featured in a montage of daring exploits of adrenalin. Watching these exploits, you hear again in a deep radio voice…

The Most Interesting Man in the World.
His precise settings are never revealed,
but he performs such feats as…

Now your hands are over your ears, as the man is tantalizingly holding up a beer.

> *...freeing an angry bear from a painful-looking trap,*

Now you are looking all around, elbows out.

"Make it stop! Stop all the noise! I don't give a crap!"

And the noise gets louder, and louder and nearly fatal. With hands over your eardrums, a new awareness is enabled.

> *When I participate with my senses,*
> *To the noise, I am agreeably complicit.*

With this acknowledgment diminishes the noise and chaos. Then the mirrored room becomes quiet, like a séance.

Each mirror then returns to reflect oodles of earlier angry scenes. Yet, silence persists here, as you think;

> *I am no longer interested in the noise of machines.*

Sensing completion, you trace a finger along the map lines, and the stone tablet under your sandals, begins to whine. You know the small door approaches you from behind.

And with this room you most certainly have become agreeable. For the Amusement Park room just activated your vehicle.

Turning toward the oncoming wall, you make sure you have made yourself, not too tall.

There's a light on the diagram under your feet, illuminating the pathway, to the next chamber suite.

The play is happening more efficiently now as you proceed. Confidence and momentum blossom as you agree to agree.

This chamber is certainly much smaller and the tiles are much taller.

There on each of the reflective rotating screens, are big images of you standing here, in simple means. Then the mirrors all turn, and the mosaic reveals – every person you've ever known, is now wearing stiletto high heels.

You notice, as you witness this watching throng, your clothes have vanished – not even a thong. You stand upon this sandy stone in bare feet. Completely naked and alone, with nowhere to retreat.

You go to hide yourself, as anyone would. And a voice shouts out:

There's nothing to cover, but should's!

And with that, everyone in this mirrored ball, drops their clothes and starts grooving in the dance hall. All shapes and sizes of women jiggling up and down – alongside naked men, their packages bouncing all around.

Some are big, some are short, and others quite wrinkled.

Aren't we all, after all, just naked underneath, people?

AMUSEMENT PARK

With your new awareness, you look beyond the bodies and skin, to see the divinity of every individual within. And the dance goes on around, and around, as the mass of humanity dances to the drums of sound.

Sensing completion you trace a finger along the map lines, and the stone tablet under your sandals begins to whine. You know the small door approaches you from behind.

And to human divinity you most certainly have agreed, for the Amusement Park room has set you free.

Turning toward the oncoming wall, you make sure you have made yourself not too tall.

The scene shifts back to the courtyard of the great stone cup. There is no way out, again, except to go up.

The map becomes again a part of the floor.

You are free to roam around the chamber once more.

The door from which you just came, has melted into the walls of this domain.

However your little trek has left the old sign looking funny.

With a wink and a nod, and with a heart so big and sunny, you turn the sign around the other way.

My

Body Is

a Temple. I

Honor Expression

In

Every

Game I

Am Playing.

And to this you most certainly have agreed to agree, for you have seen how craziness can ensue and hearts can bleed.

No longer will you be in relationships that minimize your glow, when there are bountiful possibilities to explore and grow.

There is certainly more to explore in this great stone cup, where the only way out is through and the impossible is up.

You are wise enough to know at this conjunction – the map in the center has an extraordinary function.

"There is one more wing to explore," you muse.

I am even more efficient now, I choose.

I imagine myself finishing the labyrinth with ease.
To this, I can most certainly agree to agree.

So I go back to the center and again with my hand,
Move the sand outward, for my vision to expand.

This time to the slight dismay, of my chagrin,
There's the Eye of Truth Labyrinth again.

As I kneel here in my birthday suit,
I hold a passport and a card, looking really cute.

The naked truth, I am ready to see –
To this I most certainly, can agree to agree.

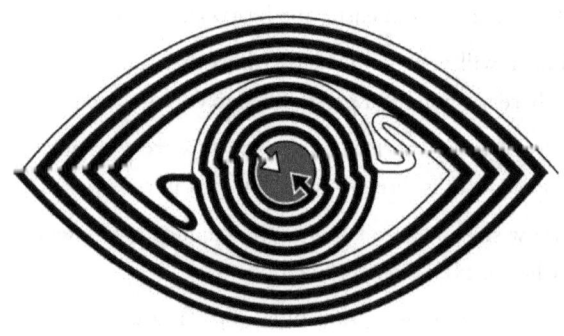

Isn't this reversal interesting?

Two arrows; one black and one white point into the center from which two grooved pathways lead, spiraling together.

Fortunately your passport explains the clue. Indeed, the next page, has the answer for you.

Page 150 - I Am Agreeable

The Eye of Truth
Labyrinth of Forgiveness.

Hold your pointer fingers to the sky.

My left is me & my right are all others, I testify.
It doesn't matter if we're long distance, or not even alive.
Our engagement has caused confusion, to thrive.

Trace your fingers from each outside
corner, left & right, one dark & one light.

I honor our individual journeys that brought us together for our plight.

Hold your fingers at the center.

You gave me a gift when we had our intercession.
It took me a while to remember — is my confession.

Trace your fingers along the opposite paths from the center.

I am sorry, and I know better now as I walk your path.
I am grateful for wisdom in our aftermath.
The character with which I played obvious games,
Is now but a shell, and nailed to a frame.

I own my experiences as learning and I start living.
I forgive you — and I Am Forgiven.

As soon as your fingers lift off of the Eye of Truth inscription, the stone begins to hum and the sand dances in encryption. Once more the floor is covered in grains. "What's below is less of a mystery now," you exclaim.

Kneeling at the center once again, you spread the sand outward with an innocent grin. This time to the elation of your admiration, the other symbol is back for re-examination.

The wing is now lighted, across from the last one explored – as the final chamber, in which to go forward.

Standing up, you look toward the map's illuminated route – on the far wall, another sign you make out.

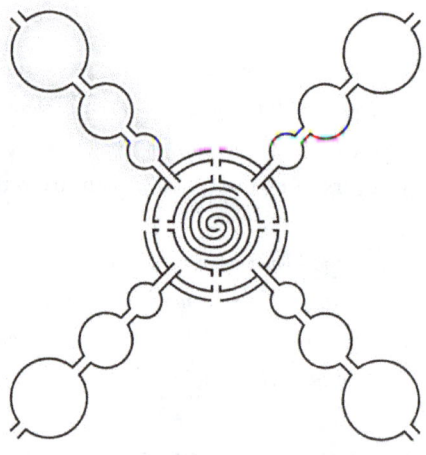

Suddenly, the map on which you are standing groans and shakes under your feet, and begins expanding.

The diagram is rising by itself to a hover. A slab of rock inches above the ground, you cover. The floor gives away and the walls begins to carriage. A narrow doorway appears behind the sign; as the next passage.

Crouching now, you see the sign. It's easy to read.

How can I hear what life wants from me?

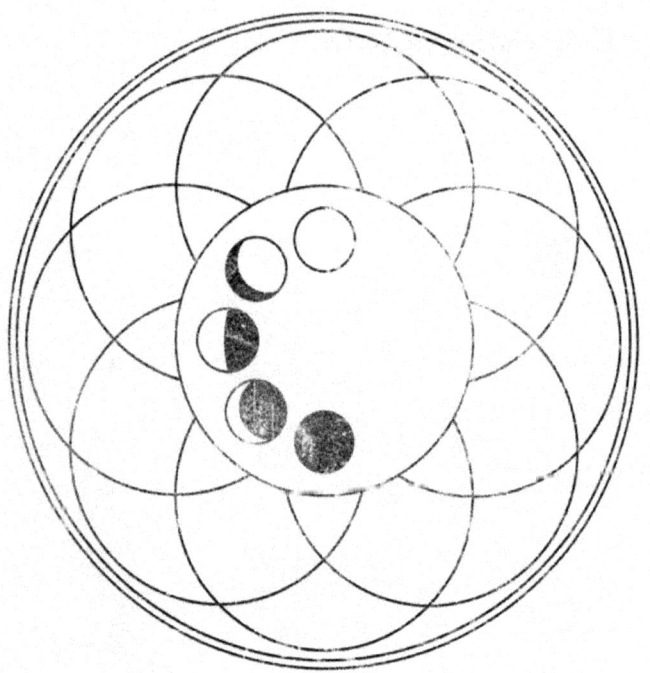

Act II
Hall of Mirrors

Scene Four:

An Illumination of Truth

Above in the sky you can feel of the fullness of the moon. It's a total illumination of the great lightened balloon. As the wall arrives, your elation causes you to dance – like a disco wannabe.

> *I wonder how I can hear what life wants for me!*

How

Can

I

Hear What Life

Wants For

Me

?

To get through the opening you bounce and bow, and to finish with power, you avow.

Now you've found yourself in the next chamber forecast. It's nothing like the others through which you passed.

The wall you just came through is now moving quite slow, so you stand on your gadget to look at the diagram below. Nothing seems out of line – only things are moving at a much slower pace. So you once again breathe into your heart, to lesson your haste.

Like landing in again an inside-out celestial ball, you are still, alone, and hovering in a galactic sprawl.

In the center is a hologram of immense goliath stature, slowly approaching. In this room you may require, a bit of light-hearted coaching.

All around you is an expanse of heavenly delight, as the entire cosmos comes perfectly to light. You are surrounded by the empty spaces of the galaxy – planets, comets, black holes, stars and moons, you see.

In the center coming closer is a floating spherical vision illuminated with all the deeds, things and people, you have forgiven. On a mannequin with facets made up of light and fabric, flashing on your old character's tunic are scenes, quite graphic.

As the holograph approaches your stationary position, you feel the pain of being human by way of transmission. The current runs through you like electric knives with voltage. The feeling in your belly is quite sharp, and revolting.

Clutching your abdomen like a soldier gravely wounded by sword, you arrive in the middle by way of checkmate move on chessboard. You know you have merged with the tunic and the center, as your entire being starts to smolder and splinter. The heat from your imagined sins gives rise to some sparks, and in the hem of the mannequin's cloth, a fire starts.

And it's over as soon as it has begun:

> *My former self just burned like the sun*
> *Rest in Peace my friend, 4 now we are done.*

Tiny bits of ash encircle your head like threads, as the wall appears in your vision and you duck your head. With this crucifixion you have certainly agreed, for the Amusement Park has set you free.

As you feel the wind of the moving door around you, you stay crouched to see what the next play gets into.

"It's a galaxy here in the middle chamber," you say, tracing the base of the grooved altar. " I am asking for help again, so as not to falter."

The Universe sensing your cooperation, begins responding to your self-reflective declaration.

All around you is an expanse of heavenly delight, as the entire cosmos is perfectly in sight.

You are standing alone in the center of space;

In every direction, pure possibility I embrace.

And now, I have nothing to fear,
For incredibly, I am still here.

And with that cosmic declaration, particles of dust begin an enlightened orchestration. The most beautiful adornments you could ever imagine are created on you, in incredible fashion.

You see yourself and you don't require an inspection. Never again will you need a mirror, as a contrasting reflection.

For the person you know you are now, is always a contribution – as you stand with what's before you; an aristocratic evolution.

Suddenly, I see, my red top hat.
And I scream: ***I Am That!***

And with this acclamation of self-devotion, you've set the Universe, again in motion. The rock under you drones and whines, and the walls again move back along sacred lines.

The room is moving onward once again, to a place you have not yet already been. With this last truth you have certainly agreed, for the Amusement Park has set you free.

Crouching down so as to avoid hitting your head, you look at the map of the oncoming stone watershed.

You are entering the last of the rooms along this line; a double completion, of some perfect design.

> *I can only kneel in this perfectly perfect amusement field -*
> *Where I suddenly know nothing, and all is revealed.*

And with this feeling of responsibility and innocence, you open your heart to what is imminent. For as suddenly as you are through the narrow aisle, you are surrounded by an expansive truth to reconcile.

In this universe, there is only light — the darkness is gone and everything feels right. At once, you feel exhaustion and fatigue, like being at the end of a long journey of agreeing to agree.

For how many times has this happened before?

> *Right as I got to the end, I required something more.*
> *Perhaps I'll just lay down here, for a moment's snore.*

So you lay yourself down on top of the maze, and close your eyes – focusing on an inner gaze. Your body is curled up in a cozy position, as you review your current amusing situation.

"First I went lengthwise on a direct route of seven. Then I completed a cross, with some kind of 14 perfection. Along the way, I saw some things I now forgive, and felt the power of creating a life I ***really*** want to live.

And now I lay here in a labyrinth, wanting peace.

How from this place, can I agreeably release?

And with this imagining, a small light begins emerging – like a locomotive converging. And the light becomes brighter than bright, taking over everything in sight. With a pop and a rush, you sit straight up in a flash, expecting to be in some kind of crash.

However it is you sitting back in the courtyard of the stone cup, where the only way out is impossibly up. Above you is a new celestial flowering; of expansive color and starlight showering.

The map becomes again a part of the floor, and you are free to roam around the chamber once more.

The door from which you must have just come, has melted into the walls of this rounded drum. You notice the old sign looking weird. You are curious what you agreed with, when you disappeared.

I am not what I thought I was,
I am, that I am, simply because.

Walking over to the sign and giving it a spin, you're amazed at what happens then. The sign reorganizes the letters, then clicks and pops – and then its bottom, becomes its top.

And just as you read the sign, it goes up in smoke and is gone in a twinkling,

I am listening with my heart, and with my heart I am speaking.

I

Am

Listening

With My Heart

And

With

My Heart,

I Am Speaking.

AMUSEMENT PARK

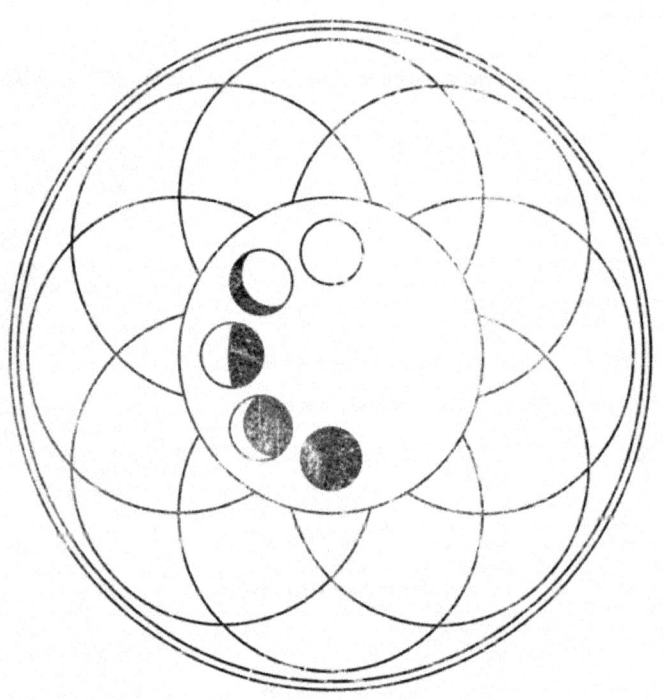

Page 162 - I Am Agreeable

Act II:

Hall of Mirrors

Scene Five: *All Rise*

And to this listening you must have certainly agreed, for the Amusement Park has set you free.

You want to know: "Is there more to explore in this great stone cup, where the only way out is through and the impossible is up?"

You are wise enough at this conjunction to know the map in the center has completed its function. You know there are no more wings to explore, or confuse:

> I Am Now Here, I choose.

> I imagine myself going through the stone walls with ease.
> To this, I can most certainly agree to agree.

So you go back to the center and with your hands once anew, move the sand outward to expand a growing world view.

This time, to the slight elation of your perspective, the map on which you stand has a rising directive.

Somehow you know to jump off the stone, onto the floor – to give the mass underneath room to uproar. You stand back in amazement, witnessing this giant bulk, come crashing onto the floor with help from the ogre, Hulk.

And the stone which is around 14 feet tall, rolls over once and then comes to a stall. From the hole that once was a map, there's a rush of some kind of gas – like when a chamber is released of its pressure. Perhaps it's a passageway, to the Amusement Park treasure.

With the map facing you as you pass by the great stone, you peer down into the darkness in stillness, all alone.

There's nothing there, but more of the same.

> Now which way is the real Amusement Park game?

And suddenly from the place you have been looking in, a fluttering happens that makes you grin.

A playing card has risen and landed on the lip of the hole. The Ace of Hearts lands at your feet, next to a pole.

"A pole – how possible is that," you say, while placing the Ace in the band of your shiny top hat.

Now looking with wonder at a shiny golden pole, you are curious if it could be the long lost exit from the stone goblet bowl.

And wrapping your arms around it with amusement, you are snatched away in one instantaneous, motionless movement.

A

I Say	Yes
To the Heart.	With all Signs
I Am Now Agreeable.	Yes, I Am Speaking

With Heart Language: For All Words Are a Prayer.
I Am Leaving Everything, and Everyone Better Than
I Found Them, For Every Scene Is an Offering. My
Body Is a Temple. I Honor Unique Expression
In Every Game I Am Playing. Yes, I Am
I Am Listening With My Heart To
All Other Hearts. I Own My
Life, And I Walk The
Earth in Peace
I Am.

Congratulations,

You've just ridden the *Hall of Mirrors!*

Keep on looking, for there's no way to get clearer.

You've ridden a vortex right into Act III.

That ride cost you one of your tokens. Was it worth it? Are you ready for more? You started with 32, now 31 in store.

The next ride *Hedge Maze of Fire,* requires 2 tokens; exactly double the last amount. You can be sure this ride is half as stout.

Can you see the equation? Don't worry, it's all working out in your imagination.

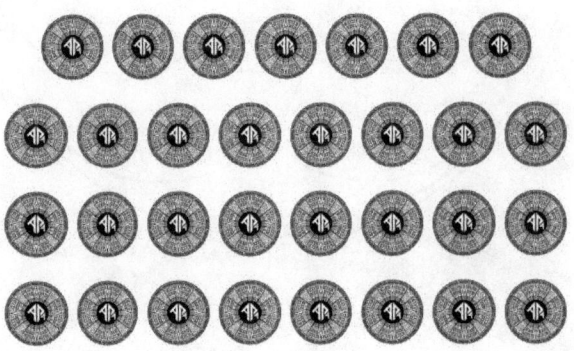

4 more rides, and you are out.

I Am Agreeable — Page 167

AMUSEMENT PARK

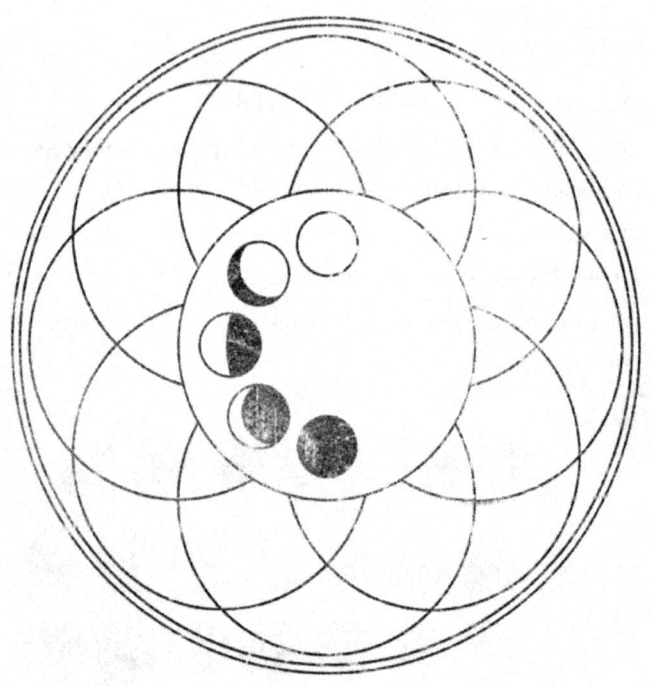

Page 168 - I Am Agreeable

Intermission:

Take Dog Medicine & Paws

Two acts down and two acts to go.
Do you want to know where are we going in our little amusement show?
How much of it is real and how much is fantasy?
Do you want to step further, into this reality?

AMUSEMENT PARK

It has been four years since Supertramp and I started our quest.

Many luminaries of the heart have come to the River House to create and rest.

We created a pocket of evolutionary and community bliss – all from our imagination while jumping into the abyss.

We feel the River House is an example of how we can universally re-tool – by riding the Arc of Resistance and banding together as a MysterE School.

Not to belabor the point, because our story really matters little at this time – for something else wants to be born from our amusing rhymes.

I want to know if we can play the same game we are playing here on a much larger stage.

Can we connect people with agreeability in a way that compassionately creates?

It is possible this book allows us a way to release our conditioning and safely untether – and does the Amusement Park have the promise then, of bringing us all back together?

I started this play with a promise – that you would be a vital part in the largest magic trick in humanity.

Yet trying to change anything is indeed, the definition of insanity. What then is possible, when we band together in alchemy?

So as you go along into Act III, consider you may have viewed your life with a bit of too much seriousness.

Perhaps the solutions we desire, are already here with us in the *not-obvious-yet* mysteriousness.

THE GAME IS CHANGE

AMUSEMENT PARK

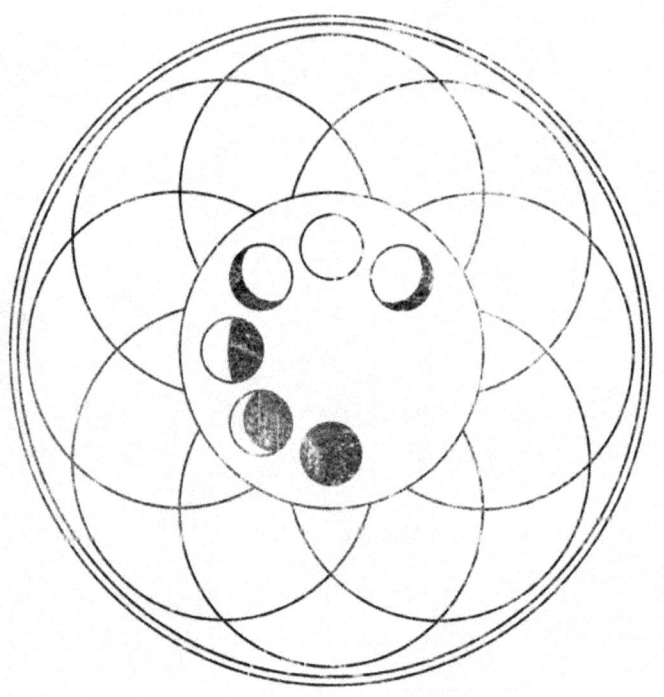

Page 172 - I Am Agreeable

Act III: *The Elemental Oracles*

Scene One: *Ready to Let Go*

High in the heavens you notice the waning of the moon. A slight crescent of darkness on the side of a great lightened balloon. Now you are noticing, you are slightly rising and whirling. The Hall of Mirrors has left you with a kind of unfurling.

You have arrived somewhere anew; gliding up the pole has given you an expansive view.

You want to know: "What just happened? Did I rise up the pole? Am I here to stay? Or did the pole simply hold me, while the ground fell away?"

AMUSEMENT PARK

> *This particular magic, is better than a variety show.*
> *What would happen to me, if I simply let go?*

So here you are, hovering all alone, on top of some great mast, so far from home. The light is brighter here for your eyes. It points in all directions you recognize. There is a crispness and clarity to the air. For this, how could you possibly prepare?

Everything is alive, and vibrating into your bones –

> *Thank goodness! I still have my clothes.*

You wear the adornments you were gifted before – better than anything bought in a store. Act II is over with cards and signs you've agreed with as intent. You're absolutely in collusion that by reading further with me, we're in consent.

And you won't read too fast, and you won't skip instructions – for reading with agreeability, allows for perfect constructions. For we've agreed to agree, while in Amusement Park, you are agreeable to this prose, until you ride away on Noah's Arc.

The memory of the Hall of Mirrors fades as you come to terms with the expanding. What are you noticing? You are feeling – a kind of enchanting.

Way below you there is a huge expansive celestial landmark. "What's that way below? Wow, that's the Amusement Park!"

All around the stone cup and labyrinth just explored, four more matrixes have appeared like an evolutionary circuitry board. However between you and there, nothing exists but air. Outside the chalice walls much lower than your perch, you oversee garden mazes – ones you must go search.

It's a fantastical expansive network of trails with four distinct sections – all of enormous scales. However, it's now a dwarf among celestial delights so far below.

And yes, I realize. The Choiceless Choice is: I must go.

No need for a map with this kind of perspective. Being above your situation certainly is effective. You see the one at the bottom has a flame that is dancing. It's obvious this is the next one advancing.

I guess I am to explore this new dimension,
As soon as I figure out my recent ascension.
How do I go about getting from here, to there?
Perhaps, I can agree to agree with walking on air?
And as soon as I say it, upon this orbital place,

A leap of faith becomes obvious – I have to take.

That's quite the risk, I might completely disappear.
What if I land on the stone floor? I fear.

My hands are tired of the holding and gripping.
Oh wow, I can feel that suddenly I'm slipping.

Only one thing left to do, and that is to let go.
The pole disappears and I fall… into the space below.

Approaching the ground, it becomes increasingly clear.
I am above some great holographic courtyard, here.

Wait a minute, there's no wind in my face!
Is this what it feels like, to fall with grace?

My clothes and hair are as still as the dawn.
As Amusement Park approaches me, by phenomenon.

The ground is falling up from beneath you at great speed. Like you've jumped from an airplane with no parachute of need. Everything is coming closer by extraordinary methods. The moment you focused your intent, away you headed.

And now it's coming closer and it's easier to distinguish. For in the Amusement Park – all control, you must relinquish.

THE GAME IS CHANGE

You wonder if it's possible to land outside the stone cup, where the only way out is through, and the impossible used to be up. And this simple intent changes your course just a smidgen, as you fly over the fiery labyrinth with eyes like a pigeon.

The view from up here is certainly magnificent. How are things going to happen in this arena, so significant?

You see in the lower maze a wandering pathway you must take — around a flame it twists and snakes. What happens when you arrive in the center? How close to the fire will you venture?

And just when you spot a solid place to land, things start to go awry with what you have planned. The courtyard below begins to vibrate and hum, pulling itself back into the place you just came from. You don't see the 14-foot stone or the gaping pit, right at the sandy place where the map once did exist.

Examining closer with the perspective of your eyes, the hole has a familiar shape you identify. A keyhole of some sort is in the floor of the great stone cup, where the impossible used to be up.

And the keyhole is getting larger and approaching extremely quick. There's no kind landing and no witch's broom stick. For in the stone cup; the way out, is through. And it's coming on fast, and amusingly for you!

You say, with nothing to do, except to agree to accept;

> *I've chosen this and it might mean death.*
> *Wait, that's like the life in which I already play a fiddle!*
> *I might as well embrace this next amusement riddle.*

The walls of the great stone cup blow by under your feet as you are now oriented towards becoming Alice's key.

As the key hole expands into your peripheral vision, there nothing to do except, brace for collision. As the blackness envelops you, there is nothing at all.

No hint of anything, and no impact of your fall.

"Where am I," you really want to know. "What happened – am I somewhere far below?" You become aware of laying on something sandy and steady. It feels like you are once again on top of the map, you know already.

> Below me is solid ground, flat with some sand.
> The passport cards are still here, in my hat's band.
> Bending down, the sand with my fingers, I push out,
> And I begin to trace the grooves of the fiery roundabout.

> Looking ahead of me, to my utter delight.
> There is another sign, in very plain sight.

> It's easy to read here from this center base.
> For the courtyard's now, a well-lit display case.

> It hangs between two posters from the Act II, show.
> *Which Ways of Relationship Am I Ready to Let Go?*

AMUSEMENT PARK

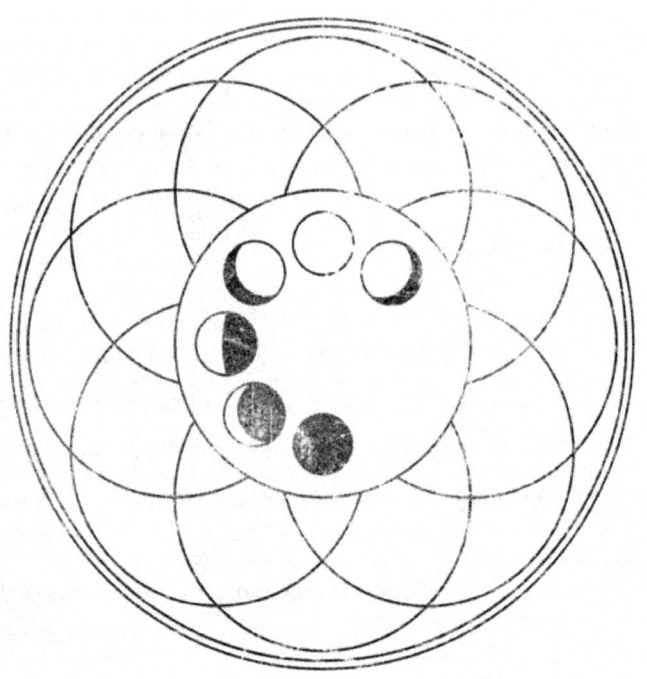

Page 180 - I Am Agreeable

Act III: *The Elemental Oracles:*

Hedge Maze of Fire

Scene Two: *Be The Light*

Above in the sky you glimpse the waning gibbous moon. It's mostly light on the side of great balloon.

You stand there looking at the sign you are just noticing. And there is something new; it looks like an opening. Suddenly, the map on which you are standing, groans and shakes under your feet and begins navigating.

Which Ways of Relationship Am I Ready to Let Go?

AMUSEMENT PARK

> *Which*
>
> *Ways*
>
> *Of*
>
> *Relationship*
>
> *Am I Ready*
>
> *To Let*
>
> *Go*
>
> *?*

Once again the diagram is rising by itself to a hover. On a slab of rock inches above the ground, you cover. Slowly and with ease, the map elevates under your ass and becomes a kind-of moving walkway path. Except you can't step in any direction at all. For where there was earth before, is now a great fall.

> *Here I go again, it's easy to remember.*
> *Time to let go, and always surrender.*

Looking above you see familiar constellations. Underneath are those seen only on vacation. Turning back toward the approaching scene, the curved walls are moving like a giant movie screen. Below the sign approaching is a narrow doorway of stone.

You know that's your entrance to the next amusement zone. Into the side of a great moving stone goblet, you flow.

> *I am going to find the ways of relating, I am ready to let go.*

Page 182 - I Am Agreeable

To get through the passage you bow, and then erect yourself back to standing somehow. Everything is bright here and easy to view. So you keep letting the Amusement Park present itself to you.

Up ahead, you see the top of a great fire burning, and before it a large hedge wall – twisting and turning.

Before you is a distinguished pathway made of grass, with walls of fabulous foliage, creating a crevasse – like an extended open aired hallway of spectacular size, flowers, blooms and smells – all coming from inside.

Mostly green density with the colors of flowering petals. The only things missing are all kinds of metals. As the pathway narrows, the foyer becomes a corridor – two perfectly aligned walls, leading to Evermore.

Once the walls reach you, your perspective narrows. It's like entering a great tomb of the pharaohs. Behind, ahead and above are twisting branches and vines. Somehow perfectly manicured into precision lines.

The walls of this exquisite botanical experience, are an arm's length from where you now stand, so curious. Growing out of the enchantment are blossoms looking whimsically romantic. The air smells of sweet floral spray – inviting you to be open and lighthearted, for miracles today.

You are curious of how this map will work, when it comes to navigating sharp twists along the cirque.

When I am standing, grounded on stone,

I trust what comes to me, from the unknown.

AMUSEMENT PARK

The stone map is still, and yet you ride with elevation. And the walls move in accordance with your location. Everything's a blended sea of jade plant climbers. *Dog-leg, right turn – up ahead!* Says one of the rhymers.

Even though this place is nicely illuminated, it's difficult to see where the coming turns are actually located. Everything is continually growing and flowing, and the walls are of the same color scheme – always showing.

You remember from your previously elevated position, this maze has corners, curves and revolutions. Suddenly a botanical wall signals the end of the line – by coming to the edge of your feet on the map, and hardly pausing to redesign.

The pathway continues onward to the right and then to the left. So the entire reality rotates around your position kept – until the pathway is again in front of you, and it moves toward you again, until the next wall is in plain view. Rotating back once more, it moves now in the other direction – the hedge has completed the dog-leg turn, in satisfaction.

Hardly did the matrix around you even paws. Seamless transition is happening; with you, not moving at all. The hallways travel toward, through and in your wake; rotating to reposition their lines – your voyage to make.

This repeats itself in a continual twisting and turning, until you feel nauseous and faint, from all the recurring.

And though you are standing quite stationary, the world is all one color with movements, involuntary. Fragrant intoxicants are inviting you to your knees. As you lower to the map, the momentum of your play, picks up like the breeze.

The jerking has subsided and the motions now are curves. The flame must be getting nearer — because you see it swerve.

The brightness of the dancing flame in the center of the maze — moves around you, as the whole Park rotates, all ways.

One moment the fire is directly behind in sight, and then it's moving around to the right. Then swinging wildly around to the opposite side, getting brighter and intensified.

Rays of light find tiny filters to sliver from within, like lasers penetrating the space you are in. The light is getting brighter and the walls are spinning, while the vines and plants move like schools of serpents swimming.

The center must be about ready to materialize. It just went by on the right and now it's quickly behind. On the opposite hedge wall the giant flame's light is flickering, as the vines and living things look like an ocean glimmering.

A right turn approaches fast, and you suspect the landscape is about to become — a fiery hot blast.

Then everything slows down and it's like 10,000 days in one. It's impossible to take your eyes away, from this blinding sun. Like a deer in head lights, you quickly give yourself last rites:

> *Well my friend, it's been quite the ride.*
> *I have so much gratitude for me, inside.*

> *Wait! I am not ready to be burnt up in embers.*
> *I have so many things yet to remember!*

Now surprisingly, you are pleasantly warm; the heat you were worried about – to your fears, did not conform. And slowly the flame comes nearer as the hedge walls fade dimmer – until, in the flames, you become a swimmer.

You feel an exotic erotic sensual sensation capable of love-making with all of creation. The feeling begins at your navel and spreads to all parts willing and able. Every atom and fiber of your humanly being – is sensing the potency of this rising sexual feeling.

You can see just beyond the outside of the fire, the hedge walls are made of plants, all full of desire. Moving and twisting and wrapping around themselves – they keep taking it higher.

Bathing in this light of love – dancing and making; the plant's very nature causes – a deep soul shaking. And as you recognize you're sharing the plant's feelings now, you internalize that all of life is one creative dance, somehow.

And it's always going on – never once fading into dawn.

And then the most soothing voice of any great mother comes into the flames and creates a buffer. Surrounded by a nurturing voice and cooling demeanor, you immediately sense there is nothing between her. And her wordiness vibration causes in you, a cellular elation – giving you quite a start…

Breathe Your Lust, into the Heart

The words activate a responsiveness; a direct shift in your spiritual consciousness – echoing and reverberating off the flames and blazing colors, the voice holds you like thousands of lovers.

Involuntarily, you breathe deep in your abdomen – for there, you feel pain, like the spike of a javelin.

What before was located between your legs, opens and travels up your spine and centers in the chest. While these flames do not burn your skin – they absolutely heat your body from within.

You become aware of sensation into the space around – feeling your true expansiveness, without any bounds. Everything you've ever suspected about yourself is true, and now's there is nothing here left to do.

Holding out your fingers – you watch them turn to ash, and rise above the flames, as everything begins to flash. Now you want to know: "Am I rising above, or are the flames falling below?" And truthfully it doesn't matter anymore, as you drift and flutter back into the Amusement Park to explore.

"First I went in the hedge maze, and turned to ash in the fire which set me ablaze. Now I am floating and purified from within…

What does the wisdom of the Fire Oracle extend?"

And as quickly as you think this – a small awareness is emerging, moving through you, like a comet converging. It's in a format of credibility, which lends well to your desired tranquility.

Honoring sexuality as the power to give human life,
is the most important of all responsibilities –
Releasing everyone into infinite possibilities.

Lust for fame, power, money and success falls apart,
By bringing my sexual energy, to the heart.

AMUSEMENT PARK

And whatever untruth, I have held inside,
Is safely revealed and purified.

Therefore, I agree to be transparent in all my ways,
And honor sexuality as sacred, in all my days.

And when I do, I find a door to peace.
So I now declare — "I am ready to release."

You must have heard the Oracle quite distinctly, for the Amusement Park has released you quickly.

You are again sitting in the courtyard of the stone cup, where the only way out used to be impossibly up. Your body once again, restored; you are free to roam around, the chamber once more.

Walking over to the sign and giving it a spin; you're amazed at what happens then. The sign reorganizes the letters and clicks and pops — and then, its bottom becomes its top.

I

Am

Telling

The Truth

And

Holding

Reverence

For Sexuality.

THE GAME IS CHANGE

Congratulations,

You've just ridden the ***Hedge Maze of Fire!***

Keep on reaching for more, there's no way to get higher.

You've ridden a vortex right into Act III, Scene Three.

That ride cost you two of your tokens. Was it worth it? Are you ready for more?

You started with 32, now 29 in store.

The next ride, ***Karma Karousel of Earth***, requires 4 tokens; exactly double the last amount.

Can you see the equation?

Don't worry, it's all working out in your imagination.

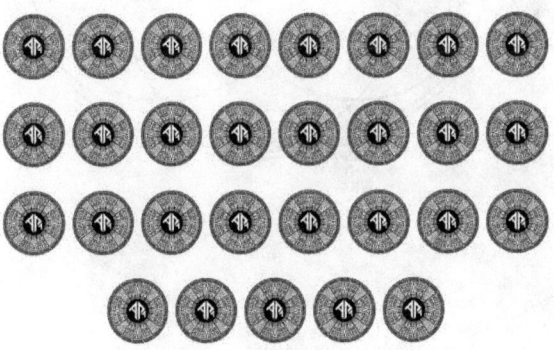

3 more rides, and you are out

I Am Agreeable - Page 189

AMUSEMENT PARK

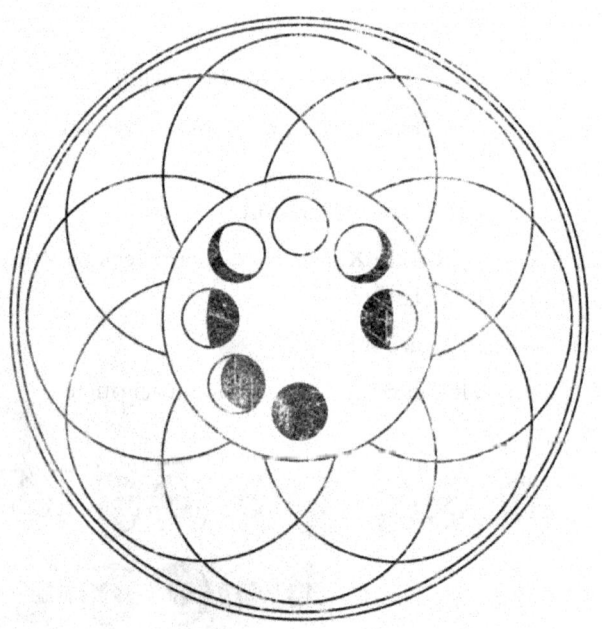

Page 190 - I Am Agreeable

Act III: *The Elemental Oracles*

Karma Karousel of Earth

Scene Three: *I Am Love*

Above in the sky, you glimpse the third quarter moon. It's half-light, half dark on the great balloon. You stand there, looking at the sign you are just noticing.

And there is something new here; it looks like an opening. Suddenly, the map on which you are standing – groans and shakes under your feet, and begins navigating.

Please show me: How am I ready to serve?

AMUSEMENT PARK

> *Please*
>
> *Show*
>
> *Me*
>
> *How Am I*
>
> *Ready to*
>
> *Serve*
>
> *?*

Once again, the diagram is rising by itself to a hover. A slab of rock, inches above the ground you cover. Slowly and with ease, the map elevates under your knees and becomes a kind-of moving walkway path in the trees.

> *Here I go again, it's easy to remember.*
> *Time to let go, and always surrender.*

Turning back toward the approaching scene. The curved walls are moving, like a giant movie screen. Below the sign approaching is a narrow doorway of stone.

You know that's your entrance, to the next amusement zone. Into the side, of a great moving stone goblet, you flow.

> *I am going to find out how to serve.*

To get through the passage you must bow and then erect yourself back to standing somehow.

Everything is darker here and not so easy to view. So you keep letting the Amusement Park present itself to you.

Everywhere are branches upon branches upon branches; a twisting and turning jungle of fantastical arboreal expansiveness. The light is held back by leaves upon leaves continually preening – making a covering of magnificent tropical screening.

And the stone upon which you are standing is flying through the canopy without hesitation – moving on the air with everything in orchestration. Wait! You want to know, "Is the labyrinth bringing me all perspectives of the tree, straight to my soul?"

And just as you've had the awareness of the Tree of Life coming to you, the stone tablet brings the massive trunk in plain view. Recognizing you are now standing on very soft earth, you bend down and run your fingers through the turf.

It's a composty, earthy, dirty, yummy and fluffy light mess – giving you the feeling of being safely tucked into your bed. So you lay down and cover yourself up with the texture, and then inhale its essence into your lungs, like a treasure.

As the fragrances implode deep in your senses, everything around you fragments, opening other dimensions. With your sight, you now see nothing but molecules – and you recognize, you are one of them, shining like jewels.

Each of these microscopic elements are carrying codes of light, that they traveled through the Tree of Life to find. From the roots to the end of the branches and back a-gain – their journey never complete, and never in vain.

While you are discovering the wisdom of being one with the Tree of Life, this movement you are experiencing is to your absolute delight. Flowing and dancing amongst all the other particles – you bounce forward like being in the best of carnivals.

And the tree who speaks from every cell of its live wood, has a voice that emanates from everything good. It vibrates deeply inside the timbers – giving your entire cellular being the feeling of flowing in rivers. And as you trickle to all the vast reaches of the tree to be fruitful – the tree speaks:

Keep Saying Yes and Always Be Neutral.

As the play goes on and on, inside this great Tree of Life – you feel like you are traveling at the speed of light. It's impossible to know if you just covered an inch, or maybe you just traveled to every leafy fringe.

The words of the Oracle have activated a responsiveness; a direct shift in your spiritual consciousness. Echoing and reverberating in the atoms with astounding viscosity, the voice holds you safe and solid, despite the speed of your velocity.

Involuntarily you witness your mind has suddenly gotten busy thinking – which is now in the way of the tree's continual giving. All about you electrons are spinning around, as you whirl and glide through this giant anchor in the ground.

Opening up your mind and speaking out loud; you keep saying **Yes!** to what's happening and it lessens the crowd. The more you say yes, the more the electrons let go of their charge – and the more you flow on, easily at large.

You become aware of sensation beyond your membrane into the space around — and you now can feel the tree's purpose in you without any bounds. Everything you've ever suspected about yourself is true, and now there is nothing left here to do.

Holding out your hands, you watch them grasp a rope. Then you descend from the canopy, saying: "That was dope!"

Now back into your body, you inquire: "Am I moving, or is the tree getting higher?" And truthfully it doesn't matter anymore, as you raise the Amusement Park floor.

"First I went flying into the forest with glee. Then turned into chlorophyll inside a tree. Now I move with a feeling to exemplify.

What does the wisdom of the Earth Oracle supply?"

And as quickly as you imagine this, a small awareness is enlarging — which moves through you like a longhorn steer charging. It's in a format of which you are certain, since it's about pulling back the curtain.

There is only one devotion of this human being.
And that is to love with all my feeling.

The place to start then, with all human healing,
Is to be united in purpose, so appealing.

Sometimes it takes sitting amongst the trees,
To hear what to do next, in the breeze.

AMUSEMENT PARK

Therefore, I follow my heart and I am always fruitful,
Continue to be safe, and travel neutral.

And when I do, I find a door that is reserved
For all those amusers asking — How May I Serve?

You must have heard the Oracle quite clearly, for the Amusement Park has released you sincerely.

You are again sitting in the courtyard of the stone cup, where the only way out used to be impossibly up. Your body becomes again restored, and you are free to roam around the chamber once more.

Walking over to the sign and giving it a spin; you're amazed at what happens then. The sign reorganizes the letters and clicks and pops – then its bottom becomes its top.

I

Am

United

in One Purpose

With

Others

Willing

To Love.

THE GAME IS CHANGE

Congratulations,

You've just ridden the:

Karma Karousel of Earth...

Keep on going deeper, for there is no way to lose worth.

You've ridden a vortex halfway through Act III. Kiva may one day let you run free.

This ride cost you four of your tokens. Was it worth it? Are you ready for more? You started with 32, now 25 in store.

The next ride *Spiraling Winds*, requires 8 tokens; double the last amount. Can you see the equation? Don't worry, it's working out in your imagination.

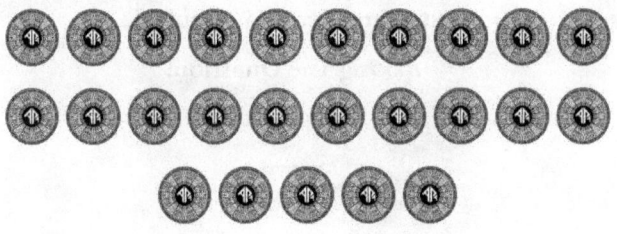

Look now, on the ground. One more card you see, face down. Glancing at it, you place the card in your hat, saying: ***I Am That!***

2 more rides, and you are out.

I Am Agreeable - Page 197

AMUSEMENT PARK

𝓐

To

My Heart

I Am Agreeable.

I am Transparent and Open

in All my Ways, Honoring Sexuality as

Sacred in all my Days. I Open a Door to Peace, 4

I Am Ready to Release. My Purpose as a Human is To

Love with all of my Feeling. I Follow my Heart

To Always be Fruitful, as I Continue to

Listen and Travel in Neutral.

Asking The Question:

How May I

Serve

?

𝓗

Page 198 - I Am Agreeable

THE GAME IS CHANGE

I Am Agreeable - Page 199

AMUSEMENT PARK

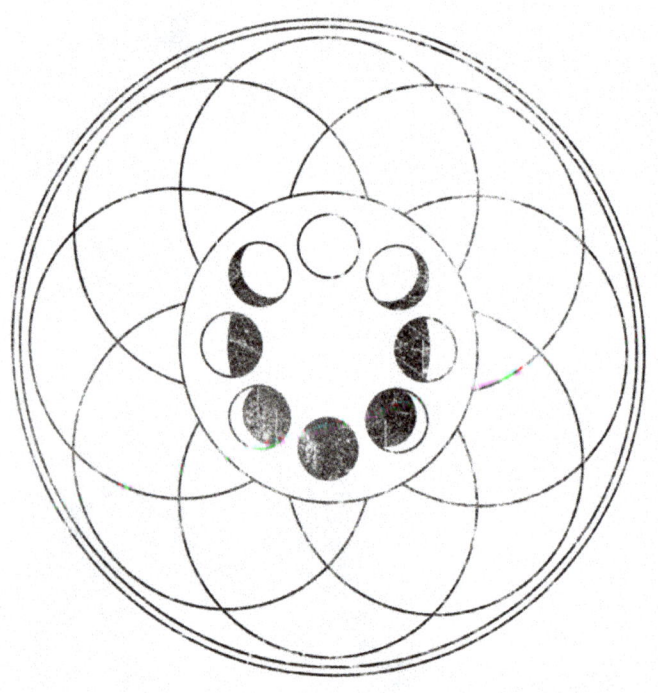

Page 200 - I Am Agreeable

Act III: *The Elemental Oracles*

Spiraling Winds

Scene Four: *BE Simple*

Above you glimpse the waning crescent moon. It's a little light, mostly dark on the great balloon – nearly the new moon's arrival. You wonder, "Am I almost through the entire lunar cycle?" You stand there looking at the sign you are just noticing.

How am I keeping score with life now?

AMUSEMENT PARK

How

Am

I

Score Keeping

With Life

Now

?

Looking at the sign you are just noticing, something is new; it looks like an opening. Then the map on which you are standing, groans and shakes under your feet, and begins navigating.

Quickly and with ease the map elevates under your feet and becomes a great howling breeze.

Here I go again, it's easy to remember.
Time to let go, and always surrender.

Turning toward the approaching scene, the curved walls are moving fast like a giant movie screen. Below the sign a coming, is a narrow doorway of stone.

You know that's your entrance to the next amusement zone. Through the side of a moving stone goblet, you move like butter around a hot knife –

I am going to find out how I keep score with life.

THE GAME IS CHANGE

To get through the passage you bow and then erect to standing somehow.

Everything is white here and nothing to see. So you keep letting the Amusement Park present its decree. And as quickly as you notice there is nothing, the stone tablet retracts under your feet and sends you buckling.

Emptiness rushes at you – as you are seemingly falling with no way to arrest the cannonballing. Faster and faster you fly through the air, with nothing in sight – but hope, wishes, and a prayer.

All around you is empty space and yet you are falling with the feeling of grace. You allow yourself to trust something new shall appear – for what's becoming of you, is happening now here.

Now the labyrinth below to the east is approaching; its walls you see upon your vision encroaching. You see the speck of your shadow as you are falling, getting bigger as you get closer to the center calling. The wind is nonexistent in your ears, exacerbating every single one of your fears.

Just a moment more of this incredible non-plummeting. You wonder "How will AP4 go about the buffering?" And now in a flash, another shadow upon the ground – getting bigger, faster, in a way profound. For one slight solitary moment you sense something above – as the darkness is upon you, reminiscent of…

Bang! Suddenly you are clobbered by something that grabs you out of the sky, pinning your arms, as you struggle to catch a breath inside. The claws in which you just have become prey, are attached to a great eagle flying away. The redirection of force left you limply amused, for it pulled you right out of your fabulous shoes. As you watch them fall into the center of the mandala grounds, you spiral underneath the bird's flapping sounds.

I Am Agreeable - Page 203

Around and around like catching a thermal; each revolution takes you higher than normal. All the while you still can't breathe – like you've been underwater for nearly a week. Grasping and clawing at the talons around your torso, you are begging the bird to let you go.

Wait! You want to know with your very last breath, "Is the Amusement Park bringing me home, or am meeting my death?" And just as you've had this awareness, the great bird loosens its claws ever so slightly, so that one small bit of air slips in your lungs, ever so lightly.

It's warm, clean and full of life force, giving you the feeling of being more grateful for Source. Then in sync with your dynamic appreciation, the bird loosens its claws ever so lightly – and into your lungs, air gets in so slightly.

And the more you appreciate what you receive, the more the claws let go – and allowing your lungs to open and flow.

And as you are discovering the wisdom of being one with the Wind of Life, this perspective you are experiencing is to your absolute delight. Flowing and dancing on top of the skies, you are cradled and cared for by an eagle that flies.

And the wind who speaks with a kabalistic inflection, has a voice that blows in from every direction – giving your entire body the feeling of being thankful in its protection. And as you soar to all the vast reaches above the AP4 to perceive – the wind speaks:

Feel Your Blessings, to Receive.

And the play goes on and on, with you in this cage of claws – and you are breathing more easily now, with cause. The more you pay attention to how you are breathing – the more potent becomes, your gratitude feeling.

The words of the Oracle have activated a responsiveness; a direct shift in your spiritual consciousness. Flapping and blowing against your flighty position, the voice holds you safe and solid despite the precariousness of your condition.

Involuntarily you notice the feeling deep inside your heart is expanding – as you imagine becoming one with a smooth landing. Thinking now in the way of the winds: you know continual giving and receiving, never depends. All around you there is up and down, as you whirl and glide above the ground.

Opening up your mind and speaking with passion, you keep saying **Thank you** for what is happening. The more you say *Thank You*, the more the bird lets go of its grip, allowing you to breathe in, another sip.

You become aware beyond the talons into the space around – and you now can feel an initiation, without any bounds. Everything you've ever suspected about yourself is true, and now there is nothing here left to do.

Taking in the biggest breath you are able, the bird lets you go from the grips of its cradle. Instinctively you open up your arms to flap your wings – discovering you can do fantastical things.

By waving your arms and motioning your hands, you quickly get the hang of flying and understand! Soaring and twisting and trying all kinds of maneuvers – you are adept at flying, by moving your extremity levers. Thankfully you are smart and you don't mess around – for now it is time to get back on the ground.

Feeling confident in your descent, you inquire: "Am I moving lower, or is the labyrinth getting higher?" And truthfully, it doesn't matter anymore, as raise yourself to the Amusement Park floor.

"First I went flying off the stone into space. Then was plucked by an eagle's embrace. Now I fly with a feeling impossible to deny -

What does the wisdom of the Wind Oracle supply?"

Quickly, a small awareness does appear, which moves through you like a herd of reindeer. And it's in a format you can easily believe, since it's all about how to receive.

The more I appreciate the simple things like my breath —
I see how complicated I let all things in life get

The place to start is my human abundance,
By focusing on my basic sustenance.

Everybody can learn to simply breathe.
And everybody can learn, to abundantly receive.

For when everyone has agreed to agree,
We shift the paradigm of all humanity.

And, we find the rhetorical question for:
If there is always enough, then why keep score?

THE GAME IS CHANGE

You must have heard the Oracle quite clearly, for the Amusement Park has released you dearly.

You are again back in the courtyard of the stone goblet, where everyone becomes a prophet.

Walking over to the sign and giving it a spin; you're amazed at what happens then. The sign reorganizes the letters and clicks and pops — and then its bottom becomes its top.

I

Am

Feeling

My Blessings

And

With

My Heart,

I Am Receiving.

AMUSEMENT PARK

Congratulations,

You've just ridden the *Spiraling Winds!*

Keep on getting started, for there's no way to begin.

You've ridden a vortex right into Act III, Scene Five.

That ride cost you 8 tokens. Was it worth it? Are you ready for more?

You started with 32, now 17 in store.

The next ride, the **Water Funnel**, requires 16 tokens.

Can you see the equation? Don't worry, it's all working out in your imagination.

1 more ride and you are out!

Page 208 - I Am Agreeable

THE GAME IS CHANGE

AMUSEMENT PARK

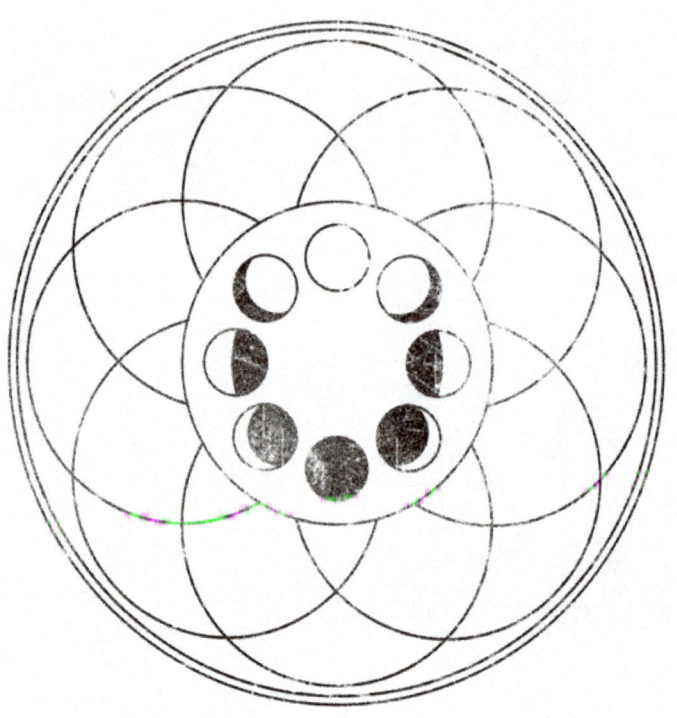

Act III: *The Elemental Oracles:*
The Water Funnel

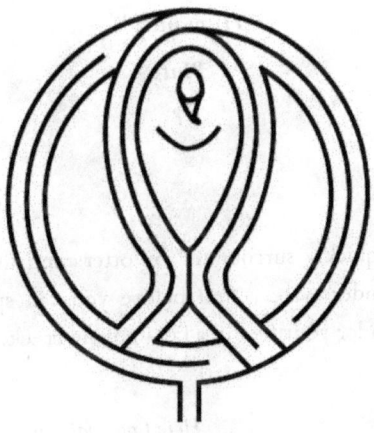

Scene Five: *Life Goes On*

Above you glimpse a sliver on side of the moon – a little light and mostly dark on the great balloon. The new moon is one day away. You wonder, "Am I almost to Noah's doorway?"

Looking at the sign you are just noticing. Something new; it looks like an opening. Suddenly the map on which you are standing, groans and shakes under your feet, and begins navigating.

AMUSEMENT PARK

What Am I

Ready

To

Remove From

Humanity's

Plate

?

The map is quickly surrounded by otters and the slab of rock disappears under water. And before you can speak, the map disappears under your feet in a fast-moving creek.

> *Here I go again, it's easy to remember.*
> *Time to let go, and always surrender.*

Turning toward the approaching scene, the curved walls are moving fast like a giant movie screen. Below the sign is a narrow doorway of stone – your entrance to the next amusement zone. From the side, water rushes to create a transition – and you say;

> *I am going to find my mission...*

THE GAME IS CHANGE

To get through the passage is easy as the water takes everything there. Now on the other side, you allow yourself to regroup and become aware.

The sky is not dark and eerily luminescent; and everything is easily seen. You watch in wonder with what is presented, knowing you will agree to agree. And as quickly as you notice you're on the bank of a large pond, the stone tablet retreats into the beyond.

A slight adjustment you make, as now you are standing shin deep in a lake. The water is warm and clear, and somehow brightly lit from under here.

The whole place feels inviting and mysterious, banked by trees and mountain fields, beautifully delirious.

You hear the slightest of angelic whispers, beckoning you to go in deeper — then the bottom drops off, quickly steeper. Now you are required to stay afloat, so it's either swim or find a boat.

And the shore which was just a few feet away, has now retracted into the background to stay. In all directions all signs of land are nowhere to be found, with not even a hint of solid earthly ground.

Treading water and looking around, you imagine maybe your luck is down. Something causes you to turn your head, and you see a piercing dorsal fin — filling you with dread.

It's a momentary blip in the beating of your heart, for what becomes apparent is a new counterpart! Dolphins swim curiously all around — you can see them looking down.

You think, "It sure would be nice to have a snorkeling mask." And immediately the Amusement Park takes on the task.

A moment later you enjoy fins, mask and snorkel — and you then you watch the dolphins, swimming in circles.

One dolphin comes near and winds around your position. It's like she is speaking to you by way of transmission. Closer and closer she swims without inhibition.

All around you now is expansive illuminated ocean. The dolphins surround you – moving in slow motion. There is an outer circle of 1,000 or more, while this one comes closer to explore.

You notice that on the back of her tail, a leaf is pressed there by the moving water trail. How strange. It's of the marine plant kind – perfectly folded over her tail and streamlined.

You wonder if it's uncomfortable and cumbersome to feel, and why is she coming closer – what's the appeal? You imagine, "Perhaps she wants me to relieve her of her problem. Now that would really be something quite awesome!"

So you choose to make a calculated move by slowly mimicking her groove. After a few moments of inching up from behind, you increase your kick to get closer inclined. But what's this? Every time you speed up your flow, the faster the dolphin seems to go.

"How is she ever going to remove that leafy snag, if she won't let me relieve her of the drag?"

So with cleverness you swim a little faster – and when you make your move, you lunge like a master. However the fish remains beyond your satisfaction, for she darted away before your action.

In frustration and physical exhaustion, you stop swimming and wonder: "Is anyone is watching?" You feel foolish and a bit out of your mind. "Did I really just try to outsmart a dolphin from behind?"

Looking outward, the dolphins are circling protective – like they are holding space for a new perspective. You are floating in a vast sea with the feeling of indignation – it's hopeful you have found this watery place to be of liberation.

> *I trust something new shall appear –*
> *for who I am becoming, is happening now here.*

Floating and grooving in this oceanic wave machine – you are protected and witnessed in the still deep waters of this scene.

And as you are opening to the wisdom of the Waters of Life, a new feeling of cooperation flows in with absolute delight.

And the water, who speaks in a hydrographic orchestral affection, has a voice you absorb from every direction – giving you a perspective of circumflexion.

The water speaks, as the dolphin with the leaf swims by trusting;

To Flow with Life – It's Better to Know Nothing

And you do what any amusing amuser would do – you laugh and giggle and allow yourself to be the fool. And in the very next moment – the dolphin swims right by you, in bestowment.

With a flick of her tail and maybe a grin, the dolphin drops the leaf and invites you to begin. It only takes a moment for you to understand – she's playing and wants you to get the leaf, like she always planned.

So swimming to where the leaf is undulating in plain view, you stick out your hand and it sticks to you.

AMUSEMENT PARK

Then pulling down the surface to replenish your air, you push it up – to go deep in there.

The dolphin is swimming a bit further behind – and you let go of the leaf, not knowing if you're out of your mind. How crazy are you to think a dolphin wants to play a game of leaf catch this way?

And to your dismay, the dolphin points her nose to the sky and disappears up there – leaving you here with a leaf in the AP4 lair.

For in this moment you are suspended in time – waiting for the next line in my amusing rhyme.

And just when everything seems lost, the stillness of your domain is tossed and shattered. The dolphin punctures your watery trip, and now everything is bubbles and splattered.

Speeding past you in delight, is the dolphin with the leaf on her dorsal, just right. Then she flicks it off her fin and onto her tail – as you recognize the mystery has just shown up, through the veil.

And for a little while, you play leaf catch with a dolphin in the ocean – your heart expanding with new devotion.

The emotions of the Oracle have activated a responsiveness; a direct shift in your spiritual consciousness. Balanced and buoyant in your soggy condition – the voice holds you safely, despite the mysteriousness of your position.

You notice the feeling deep inside your heart is sustaining – as you begin to imagine this watery place draining.

Thinking in the way of the waters – you see that the mystery of life, never, ever falters.

Opening your mind and speaking clearly with wit, "Wow, that totally was worth it!"

Then a sensation of everything moving around, causes you to feel your innocence without any bounds. Everything you've ever suspected about yourself is true, and now's there is nothing left here to do.

Bringing the surface to you and taking a big breath in; the entire scene begins to twist and spin. Instinctively you open your arms to try out your fins – and, discovering you can do fantastical things, you grin.

By twisting your arms and motioning with your hands, you quickly get the hang of dolphining, you understand! It's a feeling of absolute bliss and attraction – can we all play together in planetary satisfaction?

And though you're having fun with your new friends found – it is now time to return, to the AP4 grounds. Feeling confident in your predicament, you inquire: "Am I circling down, or is the labyrinth draining higher?"

And truthfully, it doesn't really matter anymore, as you start to spin faster through the Amusement Park ocean floor.

"First I went flying into the water with grace, then I played games with dolphins and raced. Now I am draining and spinning with a feeling impossible to deny –

What does the wisdom of the Water Oracle, supply?"

And as you imagine this, an awareness is converging, like tidal wave surging. And it's in a format you can believe in, since it's all about emerging.

AMUSEMENT PARK

In every day and in every way —
I approach life innocently, like it's my first day.

There is always learning for me,
It matters not, what I think I have achieved.

When I get off of the, "I can fix it" wagon,
I fall in harmony with what wants to happen!

Life goes on and on, in this way
For Evermore — best responding with play.

When everyone has agreed to agree
Then there's no more story, of lack or greed.

We all play together, and there is always a bed.
A nourishing meal, and beautiful conversation to be had.

You must have heard the Oracle evidently, for the Amusement Park has just released you, so reverently.

You are again sitting back in the courtyard of the stone cup, where water is dripping from the impossible that is up. You are free to roam around, the chamber once more.

Walking over to the sign and giving it a spin; you're amazed at what happens then. The sign shuffles the letters and clicks and pops – and then, its bottom becomes its top.

Page 218 - I Am Agreeable

I
Am
Recalling
Why I Am Here
And
Today is
My First Day.

AMUSEMENT PARK

Congratulations

You've just ridden the **Water Funnel!**

Keep on trying; there's no way to solve this puzzle.

You've ridden a vortex right into Act IV, Scene One.
That ride cost 16 tokens. Was it worth it? Are you ready for more? You started with 32, now only 1 in store.

And look too – on the ground. Another card – face down.
Glancing at it, you place the card in your hat, exclaiming…
I Am That!

The next ride is Noah's Arc.
Are you ready to see outside of Kiva's dog door?
With one token left over – are you ready for more?

𝒜

Yes

To The Heart.

When I Am Simple, I

Easily Breathe. I Feel the

Blessings,   And Then Receive.   Today is

Is My First Day.   There Will Never Be   Another One

Like This. I Am Agreeable to My Heart And Fall Into

Divine Orchestration With What Wants to Happen!

4 Life Always   Responds   Better 2 Play.

All Is,

Provided 4

In Every Way.

AMUSEMENT PARK

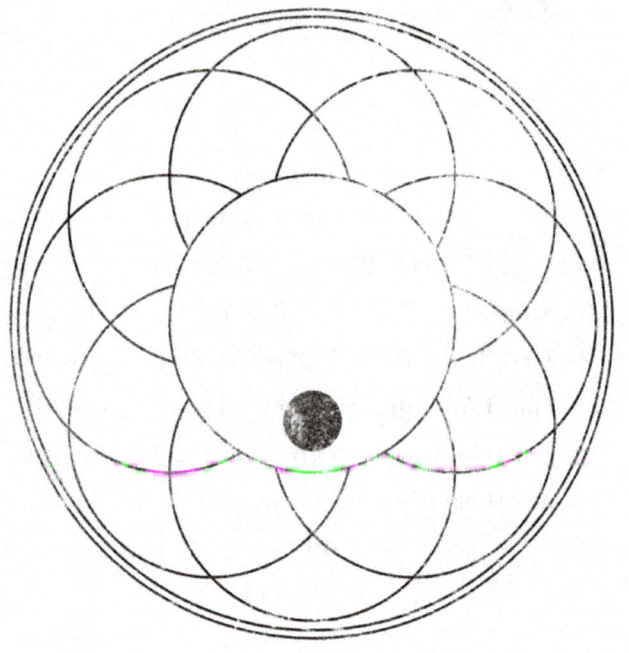

Page 222 - I Am Agreeable

Act IV

Noah's Arc

Scene One:

Above the horizon, you glimpse to see the moon. No light on the great darkened balloon. The lunar cycle is now complete – all the ride requirements of the Amusement Park, you did keep.

You are standing in the center of the great stone chalice, where anything is possible with practice. Eight signs surround you and four Ace's adorn your gallant red top hat.

You have one more token – what are you going to do with that?

Remember, I promised when you rode Noah's Arc, you'd be relieved of all agreements made from the start.

Below you is solid ground – flat with some sand. You have your passport in your hand. You are pointing at the stone map with your eyes. Is there another part of the matrix to fly?

With both of your hands you brush aside the grains. Your headlamp reveals lines sculpted in terrain. Etched into the stone from an earlier now – what does this diagram to me, endow?

Pressing your fingers into the contours and lines, you say, *This must be the last section of the Amusement Park so fine.*

The new part of the puzzle is an orbital figure eight – interlacing all the labyrinths, with energy to create.

Suddenly the map on which you are standing, shakes under your feet and begins expanding. In fact, the diagram is rising by itself to a hover – inches above the ground, you cover.

Actually, no, wait. Now, where has the ground gone? This is some kind of otherworldly phenomenon. Slowly, the map disappears and you begin to hover with ease,

as all things become agreeable with me.

I am in a holographic representation –

Of everything happening in Divine orchestration.

Turning to the approaching scene, the walls are moving like a giant movie screen. Just above your head is a bridge made of stone. That must be the entrance to the last amusement zone.

So you steady yourself as a freeway arrives – a causeway entrance, encircling the Amusement Park, to ride. Others go past giggling and dancing with delight; as you sit and watch them in your sight. They seem to be riding a kind of current; not water – but light! It stays within its invisible banks with precision, which is beyond your pay grade comprehension.

Humans keep flying by like buzzing bees on a warm spring night. You wait for a space in the traffic to pull in just right. However, you aren't sure what you are driving, or what the pick up is like. And just when you may have finally been stumped – from behind, you are lightly bumped. The Man in the Red Hat, comes up to you and says, "Hey there stranger, what a surprise. Have you been enjoying your Amusement Park rides?"

"Yes I have old friend," you most certainly say. "Now, do you know how I can get on this figure eight orbital mystery highway?"

"Well sure I do, if you take me for a spin!" And before he's finished asking, you know he's joining in.

"Join in what?" You think, "That's an amusing question." You are simply hovering here trying to solve causeway congestion. "How do I drive out of the park, and onto Noah's Arc?"

"I've just got to make sure of your agreeability," says the Man in the Red Hat. "The cards you are holding tell the story of agreeability unfolding. If your poker hand agrees with mine, then you'll get on Noah's Arc just fine. However, were you to come up a little short – to Kiva, you would have to report."

"What would Kiva do to me?" You earnestly want to know.

AMUSEMENT PARK

"Oh, let's hope it doesn't get to that," says the Man in Red Hat.

"So here is how this works: You and I will turn over our cards one by one – to see where and if, this play moves on." As he speaks a table appears next to you together; on which is a deck of cards and in front of him – a massive pile of token treasure.

"Big gambler?" You say to the Man in the Red Hat.

"Oh, I play with everyone who comes this way, and as you can see it's been a very good day."

You get a funny feeling when you place your one token down on the surface and pull the cards out of your hat with purpose.

"Oh, four cards is all you've got?" Says the Man in the Red Hat smiling. As he places five cards face down, his eyes brightly shining. "How do you plan to enter Noah's Arc shorthanded?" he asks – ever so candid. "I mean a lot of people have come through here today – but no one yet has tried a four card poker play."

"I'll tell you mate, the basics you ought to understand – for it takes five cards to play a real poker hand!"

"Well, all I found in the Amusement Park was four – I mean it is a 4-act play!" you implore.

"Then there is only one thing left we can agree to," he says with a grin. "You pick one more card and then we'll both go, ***all-in!***"

"So pull out the rest of your tokens and pile them like mine. Then, I'll deal you a fifth card, as a sign – What! Only one token is all you got? Well fine," he exclaims. "A deal is a deal."

Then he turns over four aces, all of them real.

"We've both gone *all in,* which means – the winner take it all. Let's see what you've got," he says with a drawl.

In a moment of flirtation, you turn your cards over with elation.

"Oh wow," he says. "You also have four aces from each of the suits — I wonder what fifth card, we will now both produce. For the fun of our rhyme, why don't we turn them over at exactly the same time."

"It's obvious, you've been agreeable to our Amusement Park stage — and that perhaps as a player, you have now come of age."

And with that the Man in the Red Hat deals the top card with a flick of his wrist, and the card pops in the sky and does a neat little twist. It then flitters and flies all around both of your heads — until it lays face down next to the spread.

"Flip over on three!" yells the Man in the Red Hat. "One, Two Three, I Am That!"

And with his exclamation both cards flip over — and to everyone's celebration, *both are the Aces of Earths*.

"Five Aces, an unbeatable hand! Even better than a Royal Flush! Where did you say you were going in such a rush? And where do you want to take it from here, my friend — now that you've got all these tokens to spend."

And with this, the pile of tokens splits in two and compounds in size — as everything turns into light. And like being picked up by a moving stream, your heart opens like you're flying in a lucid dream. You go giggling into the sky — on Noah's Arc, you ride.

And as you fly like particles around the Amusement Park infinity seasoning, the Oracle of Spirit speaks with a voice of ecstatic and ordinary glistening;

The Intelligence is Agreeable & Listening.

A

Grateful
I Am. For Today, Divine
Orchestration Takes Charge of My
Life. Whatever I Do, I Am Like a Magnet -
Attracting All The Things That Bless & Prosper
Me. I Radiate Love and Goodwill in My Thoughts,
Words And Deeds.   I Wish Health And Peace To All
People, Knowing the Intelligence is Agreeable With
Us All.   I Am Now At Peace With The Past, Present
& Future. Miracles Are Happening - And Yes,
A Miracle is Happening For Me, Today.
All Is Provided For Now.
Thank You.

THE GAME IS CHANGE

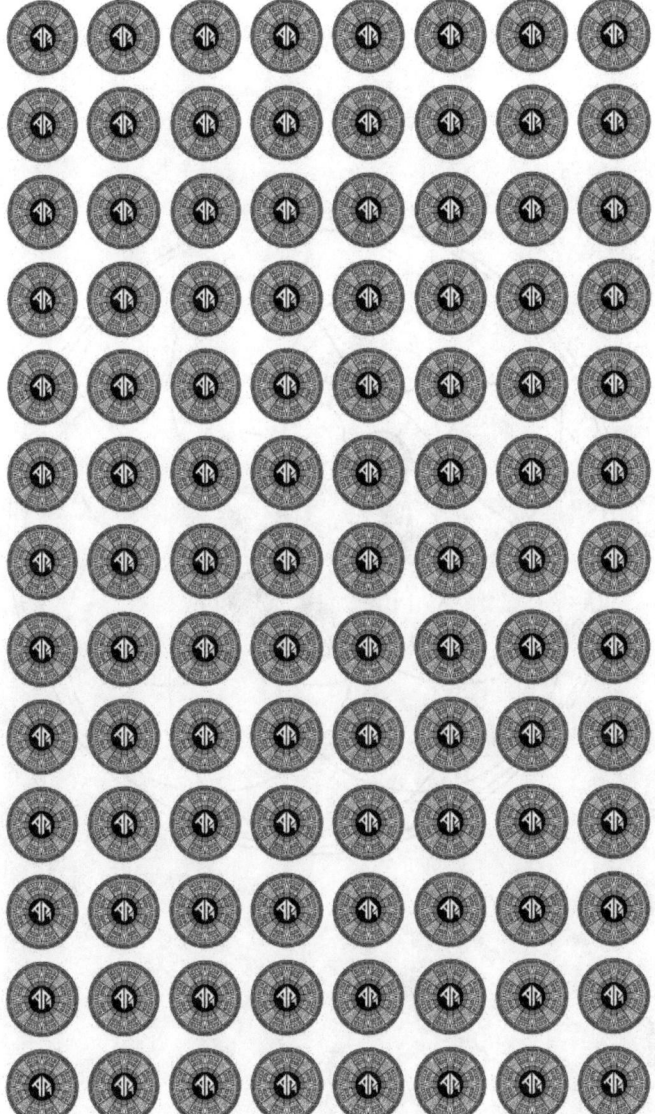

I Am Agreeable - Page 229

AMUSEMENT PARK

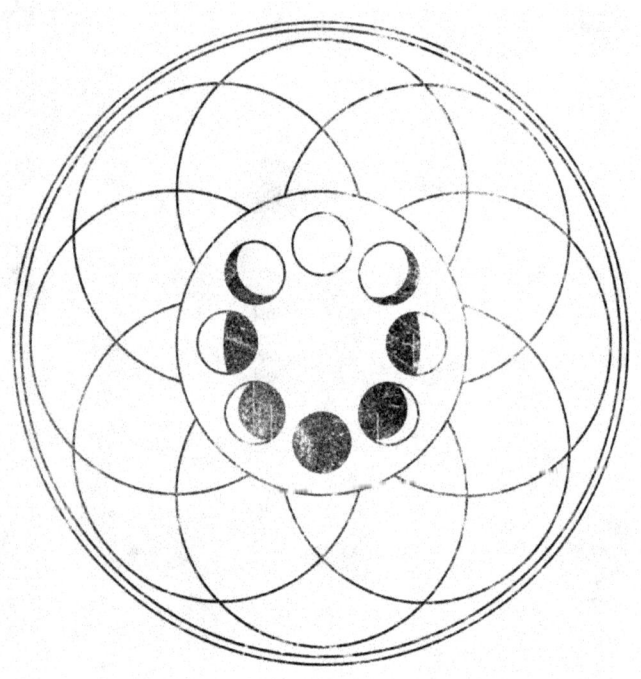

Page 230 - I Am Agreeable

Table of Contents

Introduction	**Open to The Possibility of Magic?**	**15**
Scene 1	Willing to Say Yes!	15
Scene 2	Follow the Signs	23
Scene 3	A Magic Trick	37
Act I	**Portal of Entry**	**53**
Scene 1	Remember to Remember	53
Scene 2	Let's Take it Further	65
Scene 3	The 4 Realms of Magic	71
Scene 4	Use Imagination	93
Act II	**Hall of Mirrors**	**101**
Scene 1	Oh Shit I Said Yes, Now What?	101
Scene 2	Where Are My Hands?	127
Scene 3	Didn't See that Coming	139
Scene 4	Illumination of Truth	155
Scene 5	All Rise	163
Intermission	**Take Dog Medicine & Paws**	**169**
Act III	**The Elemental Oracles**	**173**
Scene 1	Ready to Let Go	173
Scene 2	Hedge Maze of Fire	181
Scene 3	Karma Karousel of Earth	193
Scene 4	Spiraling Winds	201
Scene 5	The Water Funnel	211
Act IV	**Noah's Arc**	**223**
Table of Contents		**231**
Appendix		**233**

AMUSEMENT PARK

Page 232 - I Am Agreeable

Appendix:

For all those who are agreeable with this book, go to **IamAgreeable.com** — 4 a look. This is where we find our communal bark, and get to the fun of building Amusement Park.

Be sure those who are completely agreeable — are the ones who use this vehicle. 4 our recipe has an agreeable thread — because agreeability, is what bakes our magical bread.

Use the cards daily in rhyme — for magic tricking takes practice and time.

<u>Suggested Reading:</u>

Power of Your Subconscious Mind — Joseph Murphy

The Evolutionary Guidebook — MysterE

The Gift is Listening — MysterE

Give Her What She Wants - MysterE

𝓐

Now

With These

4 Signs I've Become

Agreeable. I Am Aware,

Alert, Awake, and I Am Ample.

So with Willingness, I now embark.

I Am Slowing Down, and I Am Agreeably

Agreeable Inside the Amusement Park. I Am

Communicating with Precision, Allowing a

Compassionate Agreeability to Flower

As I Remember,

I Am, That I Am;

My Light & Power.

I Say Yes to My Heart.

𝓐

I Say	Yes
To the Heart.	With all Signs
I Am Now Agreeable.	Yes, I Am Speaking

With Heart Language: For All Words Are a Prayer.
I Am Leaving Everything, and Everyone Better Than
I Found Them, For Every Scene Is an Offering. My
Body Is a Temple. I Honor Unique Expression
In Every Game I Am Playing. Yes, I Am
I Am Listening With My Heart To
All Other Hearts. I Own My
Life, And I Walk The
Earth in Peace
I Am.

A

To

My Heart

I Am Agreeable.

I am Transparent and Open

in All my Ways, Honoring Sexuality as

Sacred in all my Days. I Open a Door to Peace, 4

I Am Ready to Release. My Purpose as a Human is To

Love, with all of my Feeling. I Follow my Heart

To Always be Fruitful as I Continue to

Listen and Travel in Neutral.

Asking The Question:

How May I

Serve?

A

Yes
To The Heart.
When I Am Simple, I
Easily Breathe. I Feel the
Blessings, And Then Receive. Today is
Is My First Day. There Will Never Be Another One
Like This. I Am Agreeable to My Heart And Fall Into
Divine Orchestration With What Wants to Happen!
4 Life Always Responds Better 2 Play.
All Is,
Provided 4
In Every Way.

A

Grateful
I Am. For Today, Divine
Orchestration Takes Charge of My
Life. Whatever I Do, I Am Like a Magnet -
Attracting All The Things That Bless & Prosper
Me. I Radiate Love and Goodwill in My Thoughts,
Words And Deeds.   I Wish Health And Peace To All
People, Knowing the Intelligence is Agreeable With
Us All.   I Am Now At Peace With The Past, Present
& Future. Miracles Are Happening - And Yes,
A Miracle is Happening, For Me Today.
All Is Provided For Now.
Thank You.

www.ingramcontent.com/pod-product-compliance
Lightning Source LLC
Chambersburg PA
CBHW071709160426
43195CB00012B/1627